Boredom

Overcoming Boredom & Fear on
Your Way to a Better Life

*(An Ultimate Guide to Reigniting the Spark and
Building a Dynamic)*

Robert Russell

Published By **Simon Dough**

Robert Russell

All Rights Reserved

Boredom: Overcoming Boredom & Fear on Your Way to a Better Life (An Ultimate Guide to Reigniting the Spark and Building a Dynamic)

ISBN 978-0-9948647-6-5

No part of this guidebook shall be reproduced in any form without permission in writing from the publisher except in the case of brief quotations embodied in critical articles or reviews.

Legal & Disclaimer

The information contained in this book is not designed to replace or take the place of any form of medicine or professional medical advice. The information in this book has been provided for educational & entertainment purposes only.

The information contained in this book has been compiled from sources deemed reliable, and it is accurate to the best of the Author's knowledge; however, the Author cannot guarantee its accuracy and validity and cannot be held liable for any errors or omissions. Changes are periodically made to this book. You must consult your doctor or get professional medical advice before using any of the suggested remedies, techniques, or information in this book.

Upon using the information contained in this book, you agree to hold harmless the Author from and against any damages, costs, and expenses, including any legal fees potentially resulting from the application of any of the information provided by this guide. This disclaimer applies to any damages or injury caused by the use and application, whether directly or indirectly, of any advice or information presented, whether for breach of contract, tort, negligence, personal injury, criminal intent, or under any other cause of action.

You agree to accept all risks of using the information presented inside this book. You need to consult a professional medical practitioner in order to ensure you are both able and healthy enough to participate in this program.

Table Of Contents

Chapter 1: Personally Speaking 1

Chapter 2: Supplies For Beating Boredom 26

Chapter 3: Egg Shell Sprouts 47

Chapter 4: Alphabet Walk 69

Chapter 5: Birth Announcements........... 83

Chapter 6: Favorite Tea Sandwiches 100

Chapter 7: Rainbow Scavenger Hunt.... 118

Chapter 8: Heavy Whipping Cream 139

Chapter 9: Chocolate Dipped Pretzels.. 163

Chapter 10: Boredom Basics 171

Chapter 11: Why Are You Bored 175

Chapter 12: Make Everyday Interesting 178

Chapter 13: Be Curious 181

Chapter 1: Personally Speaking

Before becoming a mom, I was able to experience the pleasure of touring in the Ringling Bros. and Barnum & Bailey Circus. You heard that right. I was a clown at The Greatest Show on Earth. In the course of my time I had the privilege of meeting families from around the globe and watched their lives from a seating position at the ringside. Family members of circuses have, in many ways similar to our own family, however they are able to have an entirely different set of priorities. They aren't worried about chores like laundry, shopping for groceries or housekeeping. They just cook. These chores must be accomplished, but circus mothers aren't thinking about it day in and out. They aren't the primary priority of their day. They're passing on their family's traditions, creating memories as they use every moment to help educate and tie their families.

In the beginning, circus families educate their children about their chosen profession. I can remember a juggler that we had worked with, who was practicing regularly. He would frequently see his youngster throwing the ball up and down "practicing" beside his Dad. Today, twenty years later, the young man has been performing across all over the world in some of the top theaters with the father's assistant. They're a fantastic pair who work well together and are now not just an excellent father-son pair but also intimate family. Children in the circus are encouraged to challenge their boundaries. They are encouraged to work at a high level and mastering the new skills. One time that I can remember parents preventing children from attempting a new skill is when they could risk their life. My first time working with Ringling Bros., all guests got to enjoy private shows with youngsters from the circus. Everyone in the troupe was there and enthusiastically applauded each child's show. Following the performance, a variety of performers assisted the children on their passions. There is no distinction between ages when it comes to the roads. All children of all ages collaborate and play with the adults who they adore and strive to model. Nothing is more exciting than seeing children of different backgrounds dressed in various costumes performing schoolwork behind the scenes.

The whole world was celebrated at the stage of the circus. The holidays, birthdays, celebrations of culture, achievements as well as birthdays of animals are all reasons to have a party. This gave children of all ages something exciting to anticipate. It's true traveling isn't as enjoyable like being stuck in one spot and that's especially true if it's the only thing you've ever experienced. Circus mamas have plenty that they have in common with city moms. The majority of kids who have working mothers are able to watch her apply her make-up every day, when I was a clown, my makeup was only slightly more elaborate and included the rouge nose.

It was a great opportunity to see numerous wonderful sight-seeing opportunities. The circus families try to get the best of these. We knew that we would not see the town or even the country. When we had time off, most families did tasks and worked as fast as they could in order to visit the area. A tour around the battlefield at Gettysburg helps make it more easy to remember the events that took place at the time.

Soon after having my second baby and my spouse Jim and I made the decision to leave the circus in order to build the home of our dreams. Then I realized that my mom was consumed by housekeeping washing dishes cook, garden chores as well as endless and messy activities. It wasn't my intention to become a mom. When I met along with my fellow mothers, they would spend longer discussing the process of presoaking stain rather than spending time with their kids. This sounded like most parents view their kids as a chore that was on their agenda. It broke my heart, and I did not want to be entangled into this mindset.

The issue was brought to God during my time of prayer. He brought me back to those circus family members. The focus of my attention needed to change. Was it possible? At the night of the circus the "homes" were so small that they could be described as motor homes, trailers and even twenty-by-six-foot living rooms on trains. There weren't as many costumes because we were spending all day in costume. As the years passed, doubts arose however I was determined to fight through these doubts. I wasn't going to allow my chores to rob my children or me from the pleasure of being a mother. Each of us is just a tiny change away to make our lives better. Being a mom and celebrating my kids' lives was a joy. the life of a mother is worth the change which needed to be made. Making changes to my perspective the way I think, how I conduct myself and my viewpoint would benefit the family I love in ways that I had never imagined feasible.

I was able to share my ideas and thoughts with my fellow moms. Some of them were able to sense my enthusiasm. Creative thinking led to creative thinking. In the next few months, instead of brand the latest window cleaners, we talked about different games that we'd tried. We came across enjoyable ways to involve children into the events within our own homes. We scoured out the local landmarks as well as events would be fun for us to expose our young youngsters to. One of the best things about it was the fact that we could accomplish the whole thing for a reasonable price. Our children were happier. We were happier. Even our husbands were happier.

As they grew older and matured, I observed that they adopted this lifestyle. When something was difficult to grasp it was seen the challenge as something to be overcome instead of becoming discouraged. I observed them turning towards their friends and my husband and me to provide support and encouragement. They developed into comfortable people knowing the team at home will always be there to support them...even when they don't succeed. In the event that they fall, each of my children know that they'll have the rest us there to pick them back up.

The task of cleaning the house, for many people, can be boring. Kids get bored by when we do the chores. They become tired of us constantly nagging them to aid them. They get bored of playing with the same toys, watching the identical videos, and the same things every day. Sometime they become bored and for no reason.

It's been nearly 27 years and 4 kids since my first experience as mother. Many times, I'm praised for my "successful family." We have a tight-knit group of family members who enjoys having fun, learning while playing together. My grown children keep in touch with their children, whether they're at college or staying in their homes. My life has been a lot different throughout the past few years. There's not much I can do anymore but I'm always working, and there are moments when I want to be reassured that there's plenty of joy, excitement and happiness in my home. There is no need to view our lives as a series of time, one day after the other. We can break the monotony and enjoy these precious family moments. Being a parent is an exciting experience that we're challenged to build wonderful memories, remember unforgettable moments and enjoy enjoyable times with our loved ones. Families can be the happy thoughts that allow us to take flight. We can do it!

Joyfully,

Barbara

Get rid of boredom with a grin of celebration

Children are free-spirited creatures that thrive in the present. They excel at letting their hearts swell with joy and openness. They do not put their joy to rest. Anyone lucky enough to experience a messy kiss or hug is aware of the feeling. Children love to play with joy. They understand that how much joy you can spread your way, the more joy you'll enjoy. Kids are masters at celebrating. They do it at every event. A person who grew up having fun will discover that the days better and more enjoyable. Why should parents not join in the fun?

Shift your attention.

Everyone has heard that the work of a child is to play. However, often we forget our children's desire to play -- as well as our own desire to have fun through rushing over the play area. We hurry too much and don't experience the pleasure of living life the way it was meant to be enjoyed. Sometimes, we have to change our attention, be able to look beyond the surface to see the full picture of the world, not only this moment. It's hard to keep from letting the daily lists of things to do or appointments outside hinder us from cuddling with our loved ones, teasing and telling terrible knock-knock jokes. In reality, in the future, we'll be able to recall the knock-knock gags, but forget the things in those lists.

This shift in perspective is essential when we are parents. My good friend Ann as well as her husband have adopted twins aged two and four years old. I was told by her how wonderful it was seeing Eric relaxed because of these adorable little boys. There are hardwood floors at their home and Eric took them as fine furniture. With the addition of his children, he's moving Tonka trucks across those beautiful flooring. Being close to his kids is far more significant than the floor.

"Make everyday things unusual.

Life is an exciting experience. It is possible to strip a person of happiness. My kids get bored, and I'm bored too, so things in our home aren't as enjoyable. It's why I search for ways to make the mundane unusual.

My son Nick was just five, he experienced trouble finding things. I took Nick into his bedroom to look for something, but the next time he came back, he said that he could not locate the item. There were so many items to contemplate and consider as he walked from the kitchen into his bedroom. In truth, this made me mad. I shared with Nick the role of a detective and the way they solve mysteries and uncovered lost things. We talked about the search for clues, and then taking action. I purchased an antique fedora cap from an auction, and put up a sign saying "we leave no stone unturned" and advised him to create his private Private Investigation Agency. In the event that I needed his help to find something, I asked him to assist me with a case by forming my request into the missing persons report. He was thrilled and capable of providing more assistance to me. Sometimes, I've had to dispatch an armored knight to fulfill a task. At times, it was a "your mission, should you choose to accept it." Then, the chores became enjoyable for everyone of us.

Encourage your children to view the world around them in a different manner.

Find ways to help your children to look at the world through a more engaging, thrilling and enjoyable manner. Laughter is the gift of God that brings joy to our bad moments and brightens our rough ones. Enjoy your children. The majority of kids are hilarious.

Likely because they were brought up by two clowns, they possess a wonderful sense of humor. They are also inclined to search for innovative solutions to challenges.

Their imaginative environments become testing environments where they can improve their social skills, test different careers, and discover how to think out of the boundaries. Children can utilize the power of imagination to tackle challenges. If our kitten went up the top of a tree that was very tall and fell into a hole and fell down, I realized I was not courageous enough to get to the top of it after her. My four kids and I were the rescue team for kittens. Little ones had to be the watchers at the windows in my bedroom. my older children and I were trying to figure out a some ideas. "Couldn't we build an elevator?" said one of the children. He was thinking about how the kitten would get in the way and then ride to safety. It was a brilliant idea. My son, who was a Boy Scout, threw a rope over the limb of the tree as we lowered an unbaited tuna bucket for our kitten who was trapped. Imagined elevators became real thing.

Make connections with your kids right now.

Unexpected responses to everyday events connect family members. These become family traditions and unforgettable memories. This is the perfect time to establish friendships with people whom you could consider your top acquaintances in the future is right today. It's impossible to get this moment again. Family is your top priority.

Our husbands and me would schedule frequent "date nights" with our youngsters when they were little. When it was a date night Libby as well as her Daddy went out for a meal together. This could be something as basic such as McDonald's and then a movie. They were able to discuss their thoughts and Jim showed how a potential date would treat her. He opened the doors then pulled out the chair and retrieved her coat for her. Nicholas and I enjoyed identical evenings. I would let him unlock doors for me, and then pay for the bill at the restaurant we'd go to. Also, we rearranged our couples to a boys/girls evening out. Libby as well as me would have our hair done as Nick went to the hardware store together with Jim. The idea behind this is that you spend some time alone with every kid at least once in awhile. Relations are developed through the time you spend together and sharing the same passions and sharing moments.

With the onset of more grown-up children, we think about the good moments we shared when we were kids. We are joking about current events and talk about how they'll create great stories that we can tell over and over again. The foundations of relationships that we created during the early years of preschool have helped to build the amazing friendships that we're enjoying when our children become teenagers and early adults.

*Create memories and not be regretful.

In the bible, we are told that Mary was a woman who held many things within her soul. These memories helped her through Jesus's pain. Save things from your heart today. It was something I would always tell myself when my children were married or leave for university, I would like to keep memories and not be regretful. Woulda, shoulda, and couldas are the worst things that can happen to you. The investments I have made in my family as well as their health are yielding results since two of my kids reside in two different states. They text, call or write us letters to tell us about their experiences and learn about ours since they are aware that we have shared the same joys as well as challenges. We're connected more than the last name we have. Our history is a part of us and is not able to be erased but shared and passed down to the following generation.

- Create an atmosphere of joyous celebration.

My daughter Libby aged three, she was afraid of thunder storms. I was praying, "Lord, how can I use this to celebrate your power?" We made popcorn, then gathered around in a dark space with seating around a window, and utilized the storm as an opportunity to perform a dance in which we reacted to the amazing power of God every time we heard a thunderclap. The storms of today are the perfect excuse to have a celebration.

Our parties range from most basic to extravagant celebrations. Making a brand new flavour of homemade Ice cream is an excellent ending to our school year for us. We wear matching shirts were designed by us and then made into an amusement park reveals to our world how much we cherish being an extended family. The trip to two states for the annual Thanksgiving extended family get-together to visit aunts, cousins and grandparents will be added to our schedule every year.

Certain celebrations are unplanned and others are full of excitement. The invitation of family and friends to be part of the celebration is always a plus, but there are some things that reserved for just our six friends. There have been celebrations on the web by using one of many video chat programs. This lets distant family members become a part of special occasions and joyful events.

Get to know your kids.

The more time I have with my kids, the more I get to know my children. Whatever age they got, I was able to pay attention to them and also answer lots of questions. I was also not afraid in doing lots of explanation. I was able to get a better understanding of the personalities of my students. What really happens when they were disobedient, angry or bored? What exactly was it that caused your middle school kid decided to withdraw? Do you think that my teen is suddenly sporting an entirely new look of clothes and a lot of makeup as they are desperate to be recognized? Could it be a sign that they're in need of my attention? What limits do they have and their capabilities? Do I expect for more than they are able to or do less than is in their best interest? How long ago did they last eat? Are they exhausted? Do they get the "I don't care" message that I'm not making an extra time to spend with them? What's happening within their life? Do they require help in navigating friendships, or facing bullying? It's essential that we take time to get to know each other. Today, in an age of social media, I always make sure that I'm in my child's "friends" list. If they're younger than 18 and I know their passwords, and have complete accessibility to their profiles. The content they share and their interactions with their peers is a window to the events within their lives and hearts. It is also important to have a clear understanding of what they're happy with my posting. I also send them hyperlinks to events or articles I feel they'd like to know more about. There is absolutely nothing to stop parents from not participate in their children's lives whether on or off the web.

Make sure to leave some time unscheduled on your calendar for your child to allow them into their world. Many parents have a schedule for every minute of their child's existence. We all want our kids to enjoy life to the fullest, but at times, we must take a moment to sit with them to examine their minds and minds, and really understand their personalities. Who is the one God put in your life? Spend some time in peace for them to be attentive for a while, and spend time with them without distractions. get to know them.

Be confident about not being excellent enough.

We took Libby to a dance class close to our home. Miss Shirlene owned a small studio inside her barn. The girls danced and twirled and jumped for an hour each week. Libby was not able to learn much in dance, however she was able to appreciate songs. Miss Shirlene showed her creativity and self-confidence to the preschoolers. In the following summer, we took Libby to a highly recommended gymnastics academy to learn gymnastics and tumbling. It was to be an amazing gymnasium that would prepare Olympic hopefuls. It cost a lot of money and was incredibly bad. Libby was not a good friend did not learn much and was very awkward. They didn't even know the things that Miss Shirlene had to say. Children in preschool need to cultivate their creative skills and explore things. They must enjoy themselves and meet new people. The children must be provided with opportunities, not restrictions in their learning or life experience. It's time to be serious. can be a while away. Twenty years later, our tiny girl has a dream of performing in Manhattan.

Share your passions with your kids.

Childhood is supposed to be a joyful and fulfilling time for both mothers and kids. Be sure to share your passions with your kids. It's not necessary to be listening to "children's music" all the all the time. Nick and Libby loved it playing my older Rock and Roll cassettes. This was likely because they were aware that I would kick off the shoes of mine and dance to them. Sarah and Alex are aware that I'll sing to them with a high pitched vocal chords in my car when waiting in rush hour traffic.

Participating with your children in activities you enjoy is more enjoyable for them instead of trying to keep them entertained. My buddy Ginny was a crafter who loved to make things. As she completed projects, she would give her daughters their own materials. They enjoyed working alongside her. It was true that it was longer to finish her work however, her daughters felt very special to be part of Mama's life.

Alex, Sarah and I are theatre lovers. We've had the privilege to be a part of several shows with each other. Every now and then, I hear adult cast members telling me how blessed it is to have my son and enjoy such a good relations with them. This relationship wasn't created through chance. My husband Jim and I have invited our kids into our lives and strive to be with them for the duration of our lives. We don't want that they will follow our actions, however we are willing to show what we've done to our children. We've learned how to have fun alongside our kids, not in spite of their differences.

Nick our oldest loves history. Nick has been taught about the history of areas and even people due to the fact that Jim is a fervent historian. They are always sharing things they've both learned, or even acquaint each other with divergent views. Another link is formed between father and son.

Take note of those grumpy periods in the day.

I realized that from four up to five p.m. was not a good time to be in the house. Our kids were exhausted and bored, and I had run out of patience and energy. We all required a break to relax, but taking a nap can disrupt bedtime. Baths helped my children relax, so I made a bubble bath for them. Then, I played the classical music I like for me. Then, I lit the candles. I kept them out of kids' reach, of course. As they splashed, I laid in the tub on the floor beside the tub, and took a break. I think it was about 20 minutes, however it was amazing.

The magic of candlelight. It causes children to whisper, and tells them this meal is a special occasion. Candlelight dinners are extremely well-liked in our family. The glow of candles makes meatloaf an instant event.

Don't forget that mothers can be cranky at times also. Take good care of yourself with nutritious meals, happy friends as well as managing your time and stress levels. There is plenty of work tasks to complete. Nobody is likely to remove things from your schedule for you to take a breather, and mom must remember to take care of her own needs.

If you can learn to love your kids and the parental role, your life becomes significantly better. Keep in mind that you and your family were created for a reason...to assist and cherish each other, and to develop in your mind, heart and body. It's also the case for mom.

Find creative ways to entertain your family.

It's my job to search for new and innovative ways to incorporate ideas into our family. Everyone of us is a genius and has the potential to become the most ideal parents we can be for our kids. We were all designed by the Creator, and is an artist. The ideas contained from this book can stimulate your creativity. Meet with your fellow moms to discuss ways of how to handle family issues with a fresh perspective. Once you've got to know your kids more, you'll become more adept at coming up with solutions that will work for your kids. The Disney School Bus' Miss Frizzle says, "Take chances, get messy."

Chapter 2: Supplies For Beating Boredom

In the office, kitchen in a shop, kitchen, or any other the job gets more efficient if we are equipped with right tools. It's more effective to screw in a hole by using a screwdriver instead of the butter knife. The right tools are needed by children for learning and developing capabilities. It's also important that mom does not have to go to the shop whenever she needs to keep her child entertained. I've attempted to create an inventory of items that I've found very beneficial when the "I'm bored blues" hit. The items aren't expensive or expensive, they're just essentials. This is not a complete checklist. Once you understand your kids more, you'll know how to give them the items that they find most interesting.

Discover a new universe of knowledge - purchase an library card.

A powerful tool that can access a vast library of audiobooks, books video, computers, and books to your child. It is among the cheapest products you could purchase. Library cards are inexpensive and simple to get. The kids love getting their own library card. Make sure you have one for every member of the family. There is a specific tote bag that holds items borrowed from the library to ensure that we do not lose books that don't belong to us. Instruct your children on how to look after library books, and store the entire collection in one spot at your home.

Local libraries have access on the internet and you can also book books in advance. When I want to take a book out or view a well-known DVD I use the internet to make a reservation. So my family will be certain of receiving a reading reward.

*Stock your kitchen.

If you're planning to host an informal celebration, it is helpful to have all the basic ingredients within your kitchen. The family will be impressed and think that it's amazing that you cook up an amazing treat without any prior notice.

Here's a brief list of the things you could want to keep in your home:

flour milk

oil eggs

Sugar baking powder

Baking soda that is unsweetened and cocoa

shortening vanilla extract

margarine cinnamon

Powdered sugar yeast

Peanut butter and chocolate chips

If you have a child that is allergic to something, it's best to find alternatives for items they use. There are many wonderful gluten-free products at our local store. Nut butters, or seed butters could replace peanut butter.

Items to be saved.

Use these materials for projects. Just save a few. You don't need 15 toilet paper rolls. Everyone has an ongoing stock of these items.

Margarine tubs that have lidaluminum pie plate

empty toilet paper rolls, grocery bags

Coffee cans with lids, shoe boxes

newspaper containers for plastic drinks

* Craft Supplies.

Crafts are excellent presents for children. It is better to present supplies instead of the complete kit of craft supplies. I love to test my children's imagination. It's exciting to see what they can come up with rather than creating what's printed on an empty box. Buy good quality supplies. Crayola crayons along with good quality scissors can help to keep your tension levels at a minimum. It's difficult to complete an excellent job when the crayons are all wax with has no colour. Make sure to keep the crafting tools in a tidy, yet easily accessible location. As children, Nick as well as Libby were young, they had the permission of their parents to take the crafting materials out. It was my opinion that this was a sensible practice for our family. Determine how you'd like to manage access to the items you have.

Shoeboxes and clear plastic bins can be great storage solutions for all your materials. If you label your containers with images of your kids, they are more able to help in the event of having to wash up.

Sharpeners, pencils, and erasers

newsprint, butcher paper in the roll

child-safe scissors

Washable markers

tape: packing, scotch and masking

white school glue

waxed paper

tissue paper

Tags made of oak or cardboard

construction paper

Pipe cleaners

scraps of paper

Buttons

Rubber bands

yarn

paper plates

small pieces of material like lace, feathers and other bits of material

Stamps and a washable stamp pad

iron

rolling pin

Play dough, clay or play dough

crayons

water-based paint for posters

brushes

It is also advisable to make sure you have craft smocks in order to prevent the little ones from ruining their clothing. The old shirt of dad or an apron work well. It is possible to cover tables and floors using newspaper or vinyl tablecloths in order to guard your floors from spills.

* Dress-up trunk.

An assortment of dresses is among the items that are most frequently used at home. It is possible to purchase a big cardboard box, and let your children decorate it to serve the purpose. Also, we use an old fashioned plastic crate. Start your collection by putting together a few of your worn-out dresses as well as your husband's worn-out shirts and jackets. Garage sales and estate sales as well as Goodwill stores are excellent locations to find more things to fill your collection. A lot of stores offer costumes for as much as 75% off on the day the day after Halloween.

Here are a few suggestions to consider for your trunk

Large scarves and hats

bright shirts, bridesmaid dresses and bright shirts

costume jewelrynightgowns

Vests, wigs and lace-ups

Boots shoes

Capes and purses

Hands and shawls

Most children love hats. Find ones that represent an occupation. Firefighter, construction worker the nurse, a baseball player, football player, crown train engineer, animal ears and cape all bring to mind many hours of imaginative play.

Once you're prepared, you're prepared to fight boredom at your house. The ideas contained in this guide will stimulate your mind. Childhood is very special, and as mothers are fortunate to be in a position to experience it by our children.

Seasonal Boredom Busters

Every season is a reason to be celebrated. When I asked my kids which time of the year was their favourite, they always chose the one that we were in. It's so enjoyable sharing this world with my children who make me appreciate the passage of time. The uniqueness of every season helps both you and your kids see beyond chores and schedules.

*The First Snowfall

The very first snowfall of winter season is one of the most anticipated events at our house. It has a magical power of its own. One of the most common reactions to snow in the home of any parent is fear. What can we do at home with the children? I'm not really fan of winter storms. An anxiety-like feeling is a common reaction to the news report. I'm not a fan of shoveling snow, I am not a fan of driving in the snow. If I see the snow with the eyes of my son I can am in a snowy paradise. First snowfall, or whenever we are frozen is the right the perfect time to stop our activities and take a moment to enjoy the winter wonderland.

Snow Angels

Have you ever had the moment you sat on the ground in snow and sculpted snow angels? Did you show your children how? It's a lot of relaxing to lay in the snow and hear it crunch when you swing your legs and arms in a circular motion. It's important to stand up with care so that you don't ruin the impression made on the snow. It's true that you'll get wet but the best part is that you get into the house, change into something cozy, and then throw your wet clothes into the dryer, and relax with hot chocolate while listening to a the help of a book. We love The Wild Toboggan Ride by Suzan Reid.

Ice Luminaries

My husband Jim frequently returned home from work after darkness in winter. A particularly cold night, my kids and I needed something extra special for him to be the first person to come to his new home. These lights light the deck and welcomed the man. If the weather is perfect, they will last for some days.

Materials:

Plastic margarine containers that are empty

* Spray Vegetable coating (like Pam)

* Water

* votive candle

How do you proceed?

• Apply a the thin layer of vegetable spray. Fill with water.

* Leave outside in cold temperatures for approximately an hour.

* Once the water has half frozen, take the middle of it and then place in an votive candle.

* Set the tubs out until the ice solidifies.

• Remove the luminary that has been frozen out of the margarine tub.

The luminaries should be placed on the deck or porch or along the walkway or driveway by the lights.

When the sun sets set the candle on fire and then enjoy the glow.

Ice Bubbles

It's always fun to do things that aren't typical of the time of year. Have fun blowing bubbles on an icy winter day. They will freeze when they reach the air! It's fun trying to find the frozen bubbles of ice.

Great bubbles can be created by mixing these ingredients:

1. Cup Joy or Dawn dishwashing fluid

* 2 cups hot water

* 3-4 tsp. Glycerin (found in pharmacies)

Snow Candy

The old-fashioned dessert is a classic from the early days of agriculture. Adults can sit and watch the steaming Molasses as the kids prepare the pans.

For the equivalent of 3/4 pound of candy, you'll require:

* 3/4 cup dark molasses

* 1 cup brown sugar

* 4 9 inch pie pans

* large saucepan

* Glass 2-quart

* 6 oz Pyrex (or heatproof) pitcher

Children should make the pie pans full of freshly fallen snow. Set the pans outside to cool while you're making the pie.

Mix the molasses with brown sugar into the pan and bring it to a boil. In a medium-low heat, keep the cooking process, making sure to stir frequently so that it doesn't burn. After five minutes, begin testing the syrup by pouring some onto a spoon and pouring it into a glass filled with cold water. It is ready when drops form a solid ball within the water(245 degree F.) Put the warm candy into the pitcher to allow you to do it with less effort. The children should be given their pans of snow. Moving quickly douse hot syrup over the frozen snow. After the candy has cooled, cut it into pieces bite-sized and then enjoy.

Real Hot Cocoa

If you've not had hot cocoa that is made of cocoa powder and milk then you're in for an absolute delight. It's so delicious and rich that you won't need any cookies. We just love it to the point that we've even purchased special cups to sip the drink with.

Four servings of the food you be required to:

1/2 cup of sugar granulated

1/3 cup of cocoa powder

4. Cups of milk

1 tsp. vanilla

Marshmallows

Mix the cocoa and sugar in the saucepan. Gradually add 1/3 cup of milk until you have an emulsion. Stir in remaining milk. Heat over medium-low heating, continuously stirring until it is hot, but not at a boil. Remove from the heat and add vanilla. Serve warm, with marshmallows.

*April Fools Day

Most people don't celebrate April Fools Day or they play practical games with their uninformed people. If you live in a home filled with comedians, April Fools Day takes a different definition! This is a day for being absurd. We celebrate the art of being a comic and according to the saying "everyone thinks he's a comedian."

Dressing Up

The dress code for our celebrations is a bit silly. The children go to the dress-up bin for wigs and hats, trousers, shoes and then put on their costumes for clowns. Design funny hats by using papers, ribbons, and plates or pans and pots. Your imagination is free to roam. Everything is possible in the event that it's not too silly.

Face Painting

Kids, for whatever reason, like having the faces of their children painted. It's not difficult painting faces. Clean up is enough that they can take care of it on their own.

All you require is watercolor paint, brushes with water, paint smocks as well as an mirror.

The paint smocks must be used as it's hard to pull the color out of the fabric but it's easy to wash off the skin. It's also recommended to shake the paint containers and then give your children the caps to use their brushes. So, they have little to leak.

After everyone has been dressed appropriately, ensure that everyone in the family a moment to be the center of attention at the top of the list. Make jokes, lip-syncs with humorous songs, or perform funny tales. This is a chance for your child to learn the many "why the chicken crossed the road" comedy routines. When the family entertainment ends, you can enjoy a bite to eat and a few comedy classics.

Funny Cake is a Pennsylvania Dutch dessert that makes an ideal snack during your time watching comedy shows. The clowns of Lucille Ball The Three Stooges and Laurel and Hardy always bring our attention with their hilarious performances. The best resource for these classics of video is the local library.

Funny Cake

Ingredients:

2 uncooked, prepared pie shells

Parts of Cake: Syrup

2 eggs 1 cup sugar

1 1/2 cups sugar 1/2 cup cocoa

1 cup of butter or shortening 3/4 cup boiling water

1 cup milk 1 teaspoon. vanilla

2 cups of flour

2 tsp. baking powder

1 tsp. vanilla

Bake at 350°F. Mix syrup ingredients together and add them to uncooked pie shells. Mix the cake ingredients, then drizzle directly on syrup. Bake at 350 ° for 35 minutes or until the cake is firm. If your family members are sensitive to chocolate, substitute applesauce with the syrup to create an alternative with fruit. snack

*First Day of Spring

I am a huge fan of Spring. It's thrilling to witness all signs of spring. The very first day of spring doesn't usually mean spring for our family in the Northeast, however we rejoice in the coming warm conditions regardless.

Libby is always excited to spring since she enjoys picking strawberry. In our calendar, we draw an enormous red dot for the date we believe the strawberry farm will be open. It was common for her to write down the dates as she tried to keep her fingers crossed. I'm sure that the excitement for an outing she cherished brought her so much joy.

The spring season makes us all think about gardening and flowering plants. These two games will aid in developing your child's curiosity in these subjects before they ever actually venture into the gardening area.

Chapter 3: Egg Shell Sprouts

Materials: Playdough, empty eggshells that have the the top quarter broken off, moist cotton balls, seeds of alfalfa as well as felt markers.

Let the kids mold egg cups from playdough. Put the eggshells empty into the playdough with holes at the top. Then let the kids embellish the eggshells using markers. If they sketch faces, then they could later decorate their eggheads an "haircut." Set 3-4 moist cotton balls inside the eggshells. Sprinkle seeds on the cotton. Make sure the cotton is damp, and within 3-4 days they will start sprouting. It should be kept in a bright spot, and, as the sprouts develop it is possible to enjoy the chopped pieces for salads or sandwiches.

Flower Presses

My daughter Libby likes to collect the flowers and then press them. Her eyes are drawn to beauty even in the flowers. Once the leaves and flowers have dried completely with a flower press, she makes use of her press treasures to create cards to send to Grandma. The flower press that is available in stores cost a lot, therefore we designed our own from scrap wood.

Materials: Two square pieces of lumber (the identical dimension) approximately. 10"x 1/4" four bolts three"- 4" long and drilling wing nuts, cardboard and blotting papers (we've constructed with construction paper) Sandpaper.

This is an excellent "get Dad involved" project. The wood can be cut and drill holes into all four corners of both boards of timber. Check that the holes line to the top. Sand the wood, removing any edges that are rough. Our kids always let the children perform the sanding first, then proceed to go over the wood to ensure the edges are clean. Install the bolts into one piece of wood and bolts that extend up. Then, cut the cardboard and blotting papers to be able to go inside the press. Lay one of the pieces of cardboard on top of the wooden surface. Place blotting paper, the objects you'd like to press, a second sheet of blotting paper, as well as another piece of cardboard. There have been more than 10 layers using our press. The more material you place in the press, the longer it takes to dry. After all your foliage and flowers are inside the press, you can place the upper piece of wood onto the bolts with four extensions. Then tighten the wings nuts. Flowers should be in bloom in 3 to 4 weeks.

If you want to use the pressed flowers as artwork or cards use thin white glue and the addition of water. Allow your child to paint the glue onto the cardstock or paper they're decorating, and then arrange their flower arrangements on top. Add another layer of glue on top of the whole image. The glue will set and the plant will become secured. Forward the artwork completed to family and friends to signal the arrival of Spring.

*May Day

The day that begins May is a day of fun for us. We create baskets of blooms either real or made to give out to our neighbors. Kids love sneaking into their homes and leaving surprises. The kids ring the doorbell, and then run. They hide behind the bush in anticipation of seeing the reactions that of our neighbours in response to our unintentional gift. It's essential that children experience the excitement of sharing a an anonymous manner.

Baskets

We've made baskets from some of the most bizarre substances. Designing the most unique basket is now one of the most enjoyable activities. Plastic strawberry baskets that are decorated with ribbons. Toilet paper rolls with a design with staples and closed on one side work great as well. String or ribbon into handles by simply tying it onto the end of the. Everything is possible to paint or cover by your child's art. You can try milk containers, flowers, cups of paper and yogurt containers.

Flowers

Materials: Tissue papers, colored or white markers and water spray bottles, pipe cleaners.

It's not always easy to come up with enough flowers to fill our containers, so we've come up with our own ideas. Tissue paper flowers are very easy to make and appear attractive and vibrant. It is possible to use colored paper, or let your kids sketch on the white tissue using markers. The tissue can be misted lightly using the spray bottle of water and the colors will flow across each other to create an unique look. After the tissue is dried then layer it on top of three other pieces. The layered sheet is folded over itself as an elongated fan. Attach a pipe cleaner to the center of the paper securely. Lay out the tissue paper to create a beautiful flower. Make butterflies similarly by using coffee filters.

Flower Cookies

Ingredients:

Refrigerated Butter Cookie dough (like Pillsbury)

Large marshmallows

Colored sugar

Colored frosting

Slice the dough of cookies and bake according to the recipe. While cooking, cut the marshmallows acrosswise into 4 pieces. Then, let the kids work the edges with the sugars with colors. After the cookies have baked and cool, spread frosting on the cookies. Children can also help by helping children use an ice cream scoop for spread. Sprinkle six slices of marshmallow equally around the edges of the cookie.

Planting a Garden

May Day is usually when we prepare our gardens to be planted. Make sure to check whether it's frost-safe in your part in the United States. I enjoy digging around in the dirt along with my children. Then we put on old clothes and get right into it. There have been some interesting ideas in our garden. We've also had a garden for pizza that we had planted with all the ingredients we love on pizza, including tomatoes as well as peppers, basil garlic and even onions. My son isn't normally a fan of veggies however, the more he cultivates it is more likely for him to consume it...even the spinach and broccoli. Check out these gardening initiatives.

Flower House

Materials: sunflower seeds, morning glory seeds.

Place the sunflower seeds on a triangle with three sides with the seeds placed about 8" from each other. The morning glory will be planted between every sunflower. Once the flowers begin to grow, your kids will be able to build an all-three-sided "house" for them to play. The morning glory will utilize the sunflower's stems as the tree. You can train the morning glories to grow over top of the "house" for a roof.

Green Bean Teepee

Materials: 3 wooden poles about 8 feet long, rope, climbing green bean seeds

Make a cross-section of the poles on the other end, and secure. The opposite poles should be buried into the ground to create the frame to build your Teepee. Then at the bottom of each pole, plant beans. The bean plants should be trained upwards up to the poles. If you do not use pesticides, your kids are able to eat during their are playing.

*Summer Splash

Ah, summer! This is the time of year that the schedules are relaxed a little. I've made an attempt to relax and enjoy the lazy afternoons of summer. Do you remember when you were an infant?

The summer seemed to go on for a lifetime. It's now like it's ended with a whimper. Have fun on those gorgeous, sunny daytime. Create crafts in the outdoors, where cleaning up is simple. Learn under a shady branch Don't forget to bring lemonade!

It can be extremely hot, so prior to when our kids could go swimming, we had to find methods to cool them off. Then we saw the whole community getting involved. In lieu of using water guns we make use of spray bottles which are available from the beauty and health area of the majority of shops. The spray is gentler and does not have to be filled often.

Trike/Bike/Car Wash

We've all heard about how easy it can be to soak when washing your car, so we decided that it was time to let our youngsters take care of the "vehicles." They were each given the option of a bucket filled with water as well as the sponge. Simple, yet they were entertained and cool for a long time.

If your kids are old enough, allow them to wash their cars. You can put on some tunes for you to enjoy while everyone gets out to wash the car.

Sprinklers

Sprinklers can be a great way to entertain children. You can let them run inside and out to their hearts' satisfaction. The lawn can be sprayed with a sprinkler or the nozzle of a the hose. Attach the hose to an upright pole, and let it release the enjoyable spray flow. The kids play with music-themed sprinklers. Kids dance through the sprinklers to tunes. The music ceases and the sprinkler continues to run. Anyone who gets wet takes one turn.

Frozen Fruit

There are many varieties of fruit to make an energizing and healthy snack. You can try strawberries, bananas non-seeded watermelon, grapes or honeydew. My daughter Sarah enjoys frozen grapes.

*Autumn Festivities

The autumn season is a moment to relax following a long summer. Enjoy walks, and the changing of the leaves together with your kids. As the days get shorter, and there are plenty of delicious seasonal treats that you can take advantage of. You can rake up leaves however, don't forget to leap through the heaps before you can bag them.

Leaf Suncatchers

Materials: waxed paper older crayons, sharpener for crayons and pencils leaves, iron, the ironing board as well as newspapers

Let your children collect colorful leaves. Check for leaves which aren't shattered or bent. Every child gets the waxed sheet. Let them place the leaves in a row of four or five, according to their size onto the sheet. Sharpen their crayons before spreading shavings across the leaves. Put another waxed paper over it. Lay the newspaper down on the ironing board. Then, quickly "iron" the waxed paper using a hot iron. Once the paper is cool, it are fused. Place the suncatchers on the window to let everyone take pleasure in.

Roasting Chestnuts

Many people associate Christmas and roasting chestnuts although they're cheaper and readily available during autumn. For roasting, heat your oven to 350°F. Cut the "x" in the shell of each chestnut. Set them on a cookie tray, and then sprinkle them with water. Bake for 15 to 20 minutes or until shells begin to curl. Check one of them by inserting a sharp knife into to determine if they are firm (much as cake). Allow the chestnuts to cool however, they should not be cold before taking a bite. They are best enjoyed served with a glass or two of cider.

The abundance of apples is evident in autumn and are tasty. A relaxing afternoon of picking apples could be an unforgettable moment in time. Take this simpler than pie recipe after you return at home.

Apple Cobbler

Ingredients Include: 14 cup butter

4 cups peeled, cored, and cut into slices apple slices

1 cup of sugar

1 tablespoon.. and 2/3 of a cup baking powder (like Bisquick)

1/2 tsp. cinnamon

2 tablespoons.. Brown sugar

2 tbs.. milk

Bake at 400 degrees. In a casserole combine fruit, sugar, 1 tbs. baking mix and cinnamon. In a bowl, mix rest of the baking mix, along with brown sugar. Cut into butter until the it is about the size of peas. Stir in milk until moistened. Drop spoonfuls on fruits. Cook for about 30 mins. Leave to stand 5 minutes before serving. You can add a scoop vanilla ice cream, to make the dessert even more delicious.

Get the most value from each season.

There was once a woman who said she was a lover of each season. When winter came around, she'd complain about the frigid winter and long for spring. The spring was when she became overwhelmed with spring cleaning, and was looking towards the summer season. As summer arrived, the heat was exhausting her, and she longs to cool breezes of autumn. She was in love with every season but didn't like every single one of the seasons. Be grateful for each season that arrives. Take advantage of the opportunities you're granted. Be aware that with each new season, your child is growing older, and that's you! These days will never come again, so cherish them take them in, cherish them, enjoy these precious moments.

MILESTONE CELEBRATIONS

Preschool is the time where children are learning new things every day. It's thrilling! There's a lot to be learned and to be thankful for. If you get started early on celebrating, your child will grow up to celebrate everyone's successes. The child will be able to have many and vivid memories to be able to look back upon. Making milestones a part of their lives will build confidence in your family and provide them with a an appreciation for their accomplishments. These are the essential qualities to teach your child throughout their lives. As they prepare for them to go to college or meet with life's challenges you, they'll look back to these awesome moments from their history.

Celebrations for milestones needn't be lengthy and complex. Our family's celebrations usually aren't that big, yet they have a significant impact to my kids' attitudes towards exploring new ideas. Libby enjoyed with her brother guiding her when she was in social settings. She allowed him to answer all questions, and also make any requests she needed. In the event that Mom and Dad weren't around, Nick would take care of everything. If it came to time to separated at church, the girl cried. I explained to her that this was an important moment to take in her life. I handed her a tiny pink wallet that was made by her with her own I.D. card, tissue, and a family picture. Following this presentation I told her that we believed she was quite a large girl today. Libby proudly entered her school on Sunday the following week carrying her pink purse on her shoulder, exactly like Mommy carried her purse. Then, a few years later, as she arrived at her class in kindergarten, the purse and tissue had been moved to her backpack.

Enjoy every stage of your child's growth so that when they turn adults, they can remember their full and joyful childhood.

*First Lost Tooth

The very first tooth that my son lost caused me to go to my room crying. The boy wasn't as tiny any more; he was now growing adult teeth. I carefully wrapped his tooth with plastic, and then taped the tooth inside a baby book. To me, it represented the beginning of a new chapter in his life.

We've had all sorts of dental loss experiences. One kid lost their tooth during an exhibit. Nothing is more heartbreaking than hearing your child inform you that they've lost their tooth, while crying. In the beginning, I couldn't know what the crying came from. The tooth seemed to have gone missing and had been taken away. However, when we retraced our steps, we found that tiny white diamond.

Jell-O, Ice cream pudding and ice pops make fantastic treats to commemorate losing teeth. They're soft and cold and soothe mouths with a sore throat. It has been our tradition to offer ice cream cones to our guests for dinner in the event that one of our kids suffers tooth loss. Every now and then, it's not going to cause a dietary disaster for them.

The Tooth Fairy

Certain families are troubled by mythological characters, such as Santa Claus, the Tooth Fairy and Santa. It is up to you to determine. A lot of families put funds under their child's pillows in the event that their child loses teeth. There are some who leave toothbrushes with new ones as well as special toothpaste designed for children or a fresh cup that the child can rinse using when they brush. These suggestions promote healthy hygiene in the mouth. We know of a family who puts glitter all over the ground near to their child's bed in order to increase the fun. If you're going to let the magic in attempt to let the windows open. It's enjoyable to do a crawl into the room of your kid but not to be noticed. It's exciting to listen to the giggling of their delight and amazement when they find your creation.

*First Haircut

The first time that a kid gets an "real" haircut can be an event of a lifetime. The big barber's chair that is covered in an enormous apron, and then getting approached by someone who has sharp scissors is an absolute terrifying experience for many. Make sure you have an appropriate plan and it can be turned into an opportunity to celebrate.

Bring your kid to the salon together to know what's coming up. Try to make them stay in a seated position while you cut and cut your hair. I can remember having a the beauty salon with my little sister as a child. It's a huge aid to your child as well as the barber, if your child understands what to do.

My husband made the most of visiting a barbershop together with my kids in the form of an exclusive "men only" trip. They used to perform every week from the time Nick was born. It was my pleasure to go along for on the first trip to snap pictures and to save a little bit of the soft baby hair. This was a different addition to the baby's book. Hairdressers may provide an envelope specifically for a baby's first haircut. After Nick went off to college, Jim and Alex visited the same salon and filled the Mr. B up on the latest going on in their big brother's day-to-day life.

*Potty Training

Toilet training. Just this thought could cause fear within a parent's head. Be assured that all children are taught to go to the bathroom. There are some who have a longer time than others However, I've never seen anyone in the one grade not wearing diapers. After this is accomplished, there is a time to have celebration. The family we were with celebrated this achievement with a trip at Wal-Mart, where we could purchase "big kid" underwear. The trip was topped by having a snack at the snack store. Although it may not appear like anything, but the concept of this particular shopping experience can be all a child needs to inspire them to succeed at this level.

A mom of mine bought basic training clothes for her kids. They embellished the "big girl's pants" with fabrics and paints. The girls were impressed with their newly purchased underwear was very stylish and they made sure to wash them regularly.

*ABC's, 123's

The ABC's and the numbers is one of the preschoolers' first academic accomplishments. These ideas can be used for helping them to master the concepts or celebrate their accomplishment of these skills. By making these subjects enjoyable, learning and reading will be much more enjoyable throughout the years. Keep in mind that each experience that your child has will become the foundation for the future.

Chapter 4: Alphabet Walk

Walk with your child. Challenge you to look for objects that start with the letters of the alphabet. With a tiny notepad, mark the alphabet's letters on every page. As you stroll, your child may mark the pages with letters when they see something beginning with the alphabet. If you fail to finish the alphabet in full, the process starts from where you finished the next time. This game keeps kids engaged while mom enjoys breath and gets some exercise.

Easy Alphabet Soup

All soups could be easily converted to alphabet soup. Find a box of alphabet-themed pasta at your next grocery shopping spree. A handful of pasta in the soup can keep your child happily eating and learning their alphabet.

Letter Pancakes

The homemade pancakes we make are a staple in our household. It can be eaten consumed for breakfast, lunch, or even dinner. Pancakes are affordable, filling and are able to be made into any form. To serve the ABC dinner, I pour the batter in letter-shaped shapes. It is also possible to pour it in numbers with similar methods. It requires quick hands and a bit of practice however any mistakes are easily erased. Refillable plastic ketchup or mustard squirt bottles make it easier to pour the letters.

There are pre-packaged pancake mixes, or you can make your own.

In order to make 16 pancakes in total, it is necessary to:

2 eggs,

1 3/4 cups milk

1/4 cup oil

1 3/4 cups all-purpose flour

2 tablespoons sugar

4. teaspoon baking soda

Bring your griddle up to a medium temperature (400 to 400 degrees). If a couple of drops of water sprinkled onto the griddle make it sizzle and bounce, it means the temperature is right. Within a bowl,, beat eggs. Stir with oil and milk. Add remaining ingredients; stir just until large lumps disappear. To make thicker pancakes, make sure to add more flour. For thin pancakes, use more milk. Lightly grease the grid. The batter should be poured quickly in letters onto the grill. Bake until bubbles begin to form and edges dry. Then turn the oven over and bake the second sides.

To give your pancakes a different flavor, try by adding these ingredients in your pancake batter:

1/2 cup of apple shredded, and 1 teaspoon of cinnamon

1 cup of fresh blueberries or frozen (thawed and then drained)

1/2 cup cheese that has been shredded

1/2 cup of cooked and crumbled bacon

1 cup chopped nuts

Bread Shapes

My daughter Sarah was obsessed with making bread dough into numbers and letters while she was young. Kids can make use of these letters to mark every place setting, or write the names of family members during mealtimes. Make bread dough from frozen to make a quick, easy exercise. If you're able to spare time, and aren't afraid of the messiness, make your own dough by hand. There will be a need to provide distracting activities for children during the time that your bread is rising, however, the joy they'll experience when they can knock down the newly baked dough are worth it.

Basic White Bread

To make 2 to 3 dozen rolls, based on the form you require:

8 ounces warm water (90 to 100 F It should be as if it's just warm)

three cups of flour and 1 cup more

2 tablespoons of dry milk

3 1/2 teaspoons of sugar

3 tablespoons of butter, or margarine

2 teaspoons of dry active yeast

1 1/2 teaspoons softened butter, or lightly beaten egg white.

In a large bowl, mix 3 cups of flour sugar, milk that is dry, and yeast. In a small pot, melt butter and stir in warm water. Mix warm liquid with the mix of flour. Mix at a low speed until the mixture is moistened. In a hand-mixer, stir the additional flour until dough is pulling and away from the sides of the bowl. A floured work surface allows kids to work the dough until it is smooth and elastic. This should take about five minutes. You may need to add additional flour to get the right consistency. The dough should be placed in the greased bowl and protect it with a clean towel. The dough should grow in a warm, free of drafts until it has doubled in volume (approximately 30 minutes).

Allow the kids to punch repeatedly to eliminate any air bubbles. Make balls out of the dough to each kid. Let them form alphabets with the dough. Lay the them on a greased sheet. Wrap the sheet in a towel and then allow them to dry in a cool place between 30 and 35 minutes.

The letters should be brushed with butter or egg white. Preheat the oven until 400 F and bake the letters fifteen minutes, or till they are golden.

Tablecloths

While you're preparing your food, you can let your child set the tablecloth.

Materials: A piece of paper large enough to completely cover the tables i.e. butcher paper, tape or pieces of paper in a row, crayons.

Set the table covered with tablecloth. Prepare the table for dinner. Invite your preschooler to pick up the crayons, and then decorate your "tablecloth" with the letters which begin with each piece of food placed on the table. Example: By each dish a "p", by each cup, a "c", etc. You can also create the place cards of every family member based on the initial letters of their names.

Menus

Utilizing construction paper as well as magazines from the past, you can help youngsters create menus for your meal. You can make cut-outs of the dishes you'll serve, and place them into an alphabetical sequence. If you provide your kids with something to do during the time making a meal, it will be apparent that meal preparation is not as stressful. Our house is full of unoccupied children are more likely to get in problems than children who are active.

It's a lot of fun to select the letter of your choice and create a menu around food items that start with that sound. For example, a "B" meal may include the beef of your choice such as baking beans and broccoli along with bread as well as butter. Our favorite are "S", steak, sweet potatoes, shrimp and squash. If you think this is too much, consider whether your child is able to pick the dishes that begin with a particular letter each evening. A "Z" night might just make them want to eat zucchini. Also, we used the alphabets in the names of each child to create an appropriate menu. Libby included salads of Lettuce Ice cream Broccoli Beef, and Yams. Nicholas's dinner comprised of Noodles and Iced Cupcakes. Carrots onions, Ham, Lettuce, Applesauce and salad. It was a lot of fun to identify foods we like and which matched each other in these dinners.

It's not for all the time, but in the event that you have to break from a routine food planning mode, or to celebrate your mastery of a brand new ability.

Personal Letter Pizza

The majority of kids enjoy pizza. And when they are able to make their own pizza, it's an enjoyable project as well. The kids had to make their initials from the ingredients that we used to create the pizza. Pizza dough can be purchased frozen dough at your local grocery store or stop by an area pizza restaurant (not an online chain) and find out whether they can sell you the dough. It is also possible to make the dough from scratch at the home.

Pizza Dough

To make 2 personal pizzas with letters You will require:

1-1/2 to 2-cups of all-purpose flour

1 teaspoon sugar

2 teaspoons of active dry yeast

3/4 cup of warm water

1 teaspoon oil (olive oil has the most flavor however, vegetable oil is equally well)

Large bowl, mix 3/4 cup of flour with sugar and yeast. Combine warm water with oil until the mixture is well-mixed. Add 1/2 cup of flour until you have a firm dough. Now comes the fun part. In a floured area, have your kids knead the dough in 1/4-1/2 cup of flour until the dough is soft and flexible. The dough should be placed in an oil-sprayed bowl, then place it over a towel to cover. The dough should sit in a warm and free of drafts, until it is light and has doubled in size (about 30 to 40 mins). The children should be able to punch each time in order to get rid of any air bubbles. Split the dough in two equal balls. They can then press each ball into a greased, 6-inch-wide pan. Then, they can arrange the pizza toppings into the letters of the child's name. Bake the pizza at 400 F. for between 18 and 20 minutes. If you prefer thin crust pizzas, break the dough into four equal pieces.

After you've had the cheese and sauce Try these suggestions for toppings such as pineapple, olives green peppers, ham pepperoni cooked and chopped chops onions, made-to-order sausage that has been cooked and crumbled.

*New Baby

The birth of a new siblings or brothers within the family can be an occasion for celebration. But it is also difficult for children who are accustomed to being the only child. Involve your child in the planning and celebrations of the new beginnings of. At the time Libby was born, Nick was barely fifteen months old. I was worried siblings could be rivals and jealousy. How can you communicate these issues for a baby under two years old? Jim and I made sure not to refer to the infant by the name of "our baby" or "Nicholas's baby." We attempted to incorporate Nick in as many ways as we could when the time came to celebrate. We congratulated Nick on his move to an adult bed a few weeks prior to the due date to ensure that he did not think of losing his crib with the newborn baby. My sister and I took Nick out for a shopping trip to pick the perfect gift for his baby sister for her to say welcome into our home. Her husband and she also included Nick in decorating our front entrance with pink streamers as well as the "It's a Girl!" symbol. Giving him the feeling that being an integral part to the welcoming of this family member helped make the transition from a single baby to big brother simple.

As we learned that we were expecting our third baby, we asked our nine and eight-year-olds to assist us in choosing the name of their sister's new baby. Sarah Felicity is always grateful for the decision her brothers and sisters made.

Before the arrival of their second child the friends we have allowed our 3-year-old child to finish the room for their baby. The big brother utilized his toys to inspect all joints in the crib as well as hinges that hang on the door. Dad even made his son test the smoke detector within the space. After the baby's birth, this young boy took great satisfaction in telling everyone that he had made the room of his sister safe.

Family Time Capsule

The fun project makes an ideal gift from older siblings to a brand new baby. It's the fun part after the kids are at least 10 or 15 years old and you can open the time capsule to discover how the family looked at the time of birth.

Have the children decorate some big butcher paper. Use it to cover both the both sides of the shoebox in a separate way. Ask them to select the following items you would like to put into your family's time capsule that includes a photo from the present of everyone in the family as well as a card made from scratch or drawing of each family member as well as a unique souvenir they'd like their baby to be given by their family members. Also, you can include a brand new issue stamp for that particular year, or a coin from the year and also the front of the newspaper that was printed on the day your birth of the baby. Any brother or sister who isn't writing yet may dictate your what they believe it is crucial for the infant to be aware of your family. They can also write a greeting to your family's message.

Chapter 5: Birth Announcements

Involve your children in creating the birth announcement that is unique to share with loved ones and family. If you're able to gather the materials your children could complete this activity during the time you and your baby are hospitalized. This will assist your caretaker to provide activities for children to complete that has something to do to the big day. With white paper, request your children to sketch an image of their entire family, or a simple picture of the newborn baby as well as them. Print on another piece of paper all the necessary information:

Name:

Born:

Weight:Length:

Parents:

Sister and Brother:

Send the sheet to a copy shop, and print them back them on blue or pink paper (or mint purple or green, or whatever color the brother or sister would prefer). They are then waiting for happy older siblings to pass out to their family and friends.

*Other Pivotal Moments to Celebrate

The list of milestones for a child's development which you can organize a celebration every week. We had the "company meal" just for our entire family once our kids started to understand table behaviours. Our meals were always basic, however we'd serve it on a tablecloth as well as candles, along with our favorite food. Everybody dressed in casual clothes, and we listened to classical music to the background. Nicholas and Libby loved it so much that it was a tradition that they would repeat.

Reward your achievements and show good behaviour.

It is crucial to be aware the moment when your child is learning to look after things or to give, and also being polite and thoughtful. Make sure these occasions are not without being noticed if you want to see to see the same obedient behavior continue. All you need is a huge hug or a thank you note. I have had occasions where I've created a trophy or diploma in recognition of the accomplishment of a new ability. Write your child a letter in the mail to inform that you're proud of their accomplishments. Sending letters at them is an absolute excitement for a child. We're so used to reprimanding undesirable behaviour that we don't recognize when our kids do the right answer. My mom told me that it's easier to get more honey than with vinegar. Our kids love us and are eager to be a blessing to us. Make sure they know that the moment they show it.

Engaging Family and Friends into the act

We are awestruck by the time we spend with our family and friends. Children need relationships with others outside of their home. Friends and family are great presents you can give them. Everyone you invite to your child's life offers experiences and lessons can't be taught by you. Friends and relatives of adults offer support to your child's development. Your children's friends help your little youngsters develop their social skills, including sharing, independence and confidence in their own abilities. Inspire these connections by arranging special occasions for your family members to gather with other families. It is also a good idea to arrange things that help build long-distance bonds with relatives who reside in other states.

*Family History Day

Involving your children in learning about your family's history can give them a sense of community. Everyone loves hearing stories of the day that Grandma came across Grandpa and how the lineage of the family took root. Also, we love hearing our own family history. My kids are always excited to go through each of their "stories." Every birthday we have a meal with our baby books and recount the tale of their journey to becoming an integral part of our family. They are reminded of how unique they truly are.

Make use of photos and stories.

We're at a minimum one state from the vast majority of our extended family, and we don't have the opportunity to visit them nearly as often as we wish. I am very concerned to ensure that my kids know their family, despite being separated. One wall at our house, there are pictures of our family members, so that the children are familiar with their pictures. We talk about our experience and the stories of these wonderful family members with our children. They have the feeling that they have a connection with their families. At the time we meet, they aren't timid, but they are already comfortable since they know their members of their family.

Mini Family Photo Albums

Additionally, you can create books of the family for each child. Online photo editors enable you to make an album of photos. It is also possible to print pictures using your laptop or computer, and buy cheap photo books for every child. Photographs of family members are covered using clear contact paper prior to placing them into the mini albums, so that they won't be destroyed when they are accidentally taken out. Your child will now have an individual family album of photos to browse through whenever they wish.

Children are also an occasion to dig through those old photo albums. You can use them to create stories. I believe that Sarah or Alex can be considered the few ones on earth who are interested in listening to stories about the things I did at school in the elementary years and also about the shows I played during high school. They particularly enjoy hearing about how I used to be their years old and the way I handled daily activities. As Nick was learning how to cycle He asked me to write an account of the time I started riding my bike. The more information I can include, the better my tale. If I did tell the same story over and over again, but missed something the story, he quickly inform me. It's great to have an enthusiastic audience to the stories my family has heard a many times.

Make use of food and have fun

The family we have is diverse in roots, which means that we have various delicious treats as well as fun customs. What is your heritage? It's fun and educational to schedule a time to taste the cuisines of the nations of your ancestors.

Our heritage is Italian, Irish and German and we have a variety of backgrounds options to select from. It's enjoyable to have relatives or acquaintances who have the same country of origin. We sample different foods. Be aware that I mentioned samples. Do not expect your child to cook a full meal of the new foods. It's great when your child is able to experiment with something completely new. Alex's most loved food is the antipasto, thanks to our dinner samples.

For making the dinner extra special, choose songs that match your theme for the background. Visit the library to discover stories and games you can discuss that originate from the tradition you're celebration. As you cook the food, it is possible to have your kids design their own version of the flags of this country. The time can be a half entire day or an hour based the materials you have available.

*Grandparents Aunts, Uncles, as well as other awesome adults

Seniors, including grandparents can be a valuable resource for your family and you. They offer a perspective of the world that has been shaped by experiences. If you are not fortunate enough to have grandparents living Tell them about the experiences you had with them. Bring photos and other mementos to your children to create an emotional connection with the individuals from their own family that helped shape the person you have become. My dad died in the year Libby was only five years old. My children were never able to build a bond with him as his last days were spent in a care home for people with Alzheimer's disease. I try to ensure they get to know about him via me. There's so much of me dad that I observe in my kids. I remind them they are a part of the family. Libby and Alex's enthusiasm for drawing, Sarah's method of being a good friend to others, and Nick's love of electronic gadgets and collecting coins were all things that they had in common with Grandpa. This gives them a strong bond to my family and to their roots.

Additionally, I seek out older adults who can fill in my role as a grandparent to my kids. It is crucial for kids to be able to establish relationships across generations. Discover interests that your kids can be able to share with their grandparents as well as other adults of a similar age. Give the right equipment, experiences as well as education to allow your children to explore those passions. Libby is a great fan of art. She was in preschool when she discovered that my uncle Ben was an architect who retired who would create gorgeous scenes. The relationship was wonderful that was in the process of being formed. I accompanied Libby on a trip to the library, where she obtained some great art books. We bought some art supplies as well as other materials for her to use for an anniversary present. While visiting Uncle Ben there was many things to talk about and discuss. The two artists worked side by side inside his basement which later became an art studio. They enjoyed their visits and I could only imagine the wisdom from the past handed down by generation to generation as the paint flitted.

Audio Recordings

Children are fascinated by hearing about their grandma's story as much as Grandma enjoys hearing about her grandkids. It is a good idea to encourage grandparents to record the stories of their families and favourite books for grandchildren to listen to even when they're not with them. Blank tapes and tape recorders make wonderful presents for parents and kids. Kids can write your "letters" to Grandpa -as well as in reverse! Grandpa is not the only one to receive updates, but the audio effects also.

Using Artwork

Kids create more art than parents know what to do with it. It's a shame to throw it out, but it's impossible to keep everything. How do we proceed? Make use of the pictures with finger paint and drawings with crayons for stationary. The art of letter writing is dying art form that's not very sad. What an amazing treat to receive something through the mail, but not the form of a bill. Calls can be swift and simple however, what do you get to do with the letters? They can be reread, and enjoyed. Write more letters to family members and do not forget to give a few of your precious art work with people who cherish your kids. Your work will surely be appreciated as well when your child comes to Aunt Mary's house, and they see their work displayed on the fridge you will be so happy.

*Friendship Tea

It is likely that everyone will remember the time when there was a place within the community where children would gather. The house was where mother's with a childlike heart resided. There was no issue with mess or the noise so it helped her kids develop their imagination as well as relationships with each other. While I was pregnant my first child, I decided that I wanted my home to become the place where people gather in the neighborhood. What I did not realize then was how much work it was going to need to put in. It isn't always easy. my creative thinking and perseverance. I've learned to cut back and create manageable but enjoyable playing dates for my children. I learned about the kinds of games children enjoy and want to repeat over and over again.

Little girls (and larger ones, too) enjoy tea celebrations. It was my experience that if Libby has a girl friend for a visit or have a tea party, having a tea-party for food or lunch would be the perfect occasion. The event was so well-loved that it was worthwhile to invest in the right props. If your child is petite, ranging from two to three years old then you'll likely want to invest in an inexpensive play tea set. Girls who are older feel more valued when you use authentic china. Libby and I ventured to the garage sale to buy pretty cups as well as saucers, creamer sugar bowls, and even teapots. If you're concerned about your daughters breaking items or getting cut, Corelle dishes are unbreakable yet they're "grown-up." We only bought enough plates for two girls. Tea seems to be most effective in a group of two girls and not a group.

When Libby's best friend Liza was visiting, I made muffins for her and Libby wanted to know if she could host a tea party. If I told her I'd notify them when the tea was time, they happily walked into Libby's bedroom. After a short time, they came back and were evident that they'd gone through the costume boxes and had prepared for the event. There was no need to explain to the guests how to throw an tea party, or how to plan it as an occasion, it all came from the heart and put me in enjoying the atmosphere. I pulled out my teacups and brewed an uncaffeinated cup of tea in a teapot and put the tables up to serve my guests. Grapes, muffins, as well as small sandwich sandwiches of cream cheese and jelly complete the dinner. The girls exhibited their good manners, and were entertained throughout the duration of an hour or more.

Alex and Sarah created a every week "teatime" with their Uncle Peter. It was an enormous help for me to take them off for a couple of hours to garden and enjoyed their tea. It was a routine affair for more than six years. In that time, they formed an incredible relationship with their uncle. One which they treasure as young adult.

Here are some tasty treats that you can try with your next cup of tea.

Chocolate Chip Muffins

It's by far the most popular snack at our home.

In order to make 12 muffins, you'll be required to:

2 cups flour

1 cup of sugar

Three teaspoons baking soda

3/4 cup milk

1/3 cup oil

1 egg

1 cup of chocolate chip

Pre-heat the oven to 400°F. Prepare 12 muffin cups with oil or use baking cups to line them. Mix the flour, sugar baking powder, chocolate chips in a big bowl. Create a hole within the dry ingredients. Add milk as well as oil, egg, and. In one go. Mix until dry ingredients are all at once. Mix until moistened. Fill the muffin cups with batter 2/3 full. Bake at 400°F during 15 minutes, or to golden in color. Let cool for 1 minute prior to removing from the pan.

Vanilla or Almond Milk

If you're not comfortable serving tea to children Consider the milk with a flavor.

Each cup will require:

1 cup milk

One teaspoon sugar

1 teaspoon vanilla flavoring or almond flavoring

The milk should be warm in a pan or microwave for a few seconds to get rid of the chill. Mix in the sugar and flavors. If you've got a milk blender, this makes the sauce even more creamy and delicious. Enjoy!

Chapter 6: Favorite Tea Sandwiches

Tea sandwiches are small and delicate. To make a sandwich, remove the crusts from two bread slices. The bread is flattened slightly using an edging pin. Spread a thin layer of the sandwich fixings you like and cut it into fun shapes with cookie cutters. Jelly and cream cheese, egg salad as well as tuna salad and tomatoes and lettuce are among the most requested items on the tea menu.

More Tea Activities

The tea theme for planning the entire day's activities which culminates in the final tea. You can have your guests prepare placemats, table cards as well as a centerpiece for the table. They can also decorate their the hats they wear to.

Create fun and simple placemats and cards, provide teatime friends using craft paper, stamps crayons, scraps of fabric and lace, glue as well as stickers. To make the centerpiece, you can provide an assortment of fake flowers (or real ones if your gardening space has them) and a vase with lace and ribbons. For the hats, glue as well as flowers, lace ribbons and maybe some gems or beads. Kids will always use their creative ideas. It's exciting to see what they come up with independently.

I utilized the recipe for tea to help me teach my children as well as their classmates how to prepare the table. Perhaps you'd like include them in making your snack items. Keep in mind that any of these tasks may be as complicated or easy in the way you want to create these.

Being A Good Neighbor

It is important that children be aware that they are a an integral part of the community. I plan out events that educate my kids about their neighborhood and the individuals who reside in it and are part of it, as well as their responsibilities to them.

Walking across the street can be the first step in the education. It's important for children to understand how to navigate through their area and know who to communicate with in the event they are lost.

Who are the people who work in this office?

While you go to the grocery store, post office or service center, as well as cleaners, talk to your child about the types of jobs they perform and what we can do to help their services. Find easy ways for you and your children to tell them how much you value their help.

Our children love our postal carrier. "Aunt Lucy" would often receive a letter from them at the mailbox of our house when she visited. In the winter months when it's snowy and cold, we've left some cookies as well as the thermos of hot cocoa to her. We're grateful to her for her contribution to keep our community going smoothly.

Secret Angels

It's exciting to perform acts of kindness in the privacy of your home or simply to surprise your friends and neighbors. You can think of small acts that you and your kids can perform for those who are close to your home. Making leaves, sending cards leave treats, and leaving flowers are enjoyable and in the capabilities of every child (or adults).

Friendship Fudge

This recipe for fudge is easy to make. The flavor is also delicious and the neighbors, postal carriers and oilman, as well as the recipient of this recipe will thank your efforts. One recipe of fudge can go quite a distance, which means you'll be able to make plenty for gift-givers too.

For a single batch of fudge it will require:

1 cup of unsweetened cocoa

2 lbs of powdered sugar

1 cup margarine or butter

1/2 cup milk

2 teaspoons vanilla

Mix the cocoa powder and sugar together in a large, microwave-safe bowl. While stirring, mix in butter, milk or margarine. The microwave should be on high for about 5 minutes or until the butter has melted (5 5 minutes). Mix in the vanilla, and mix until it is completely smooth. Let the children help put the mix in the baking pan that has been greased. Then, chill until the mixture is dry (we normally put the mixture in the fridge overnight). Slice into pieces, then put them in small boxes or baskets. Or just plain plates of paper covered with beautiful papers.

Talent Shows

Most young children are natural performers. They are in a place in which they're completely free. If they are in an establishment and immediately move and bop. It's a means to express their happiness. I would like everyone to remain committed to this imaginative avenue. What better way to provide a chance for your family to enjoy one another? Invite the children's classmates or invite family members to join in the fun. Bring costumes, music along with some instruments and the event will handle the rest.

Easy Instruments

The most basic instruments are pans and pots to drum and funnels to play horns but if you'd like to add more entertainment, allow your young musicians to make their own noise makers.

In order to get an original one, you must collect:

Funnel

Ribbons, streamers or ribbons

empty toilet paper, or roll of paper towels

Several empty plastic bottles

Aluminum pie plates or tin pie plates

empty oatmeal boxes

New pencils that are not sharpened

shoeboxes

Rubber bands

Large beans

rice

glue

Colorful paper

tape

crayons

yarn

Buttons

Tambourine

A child of any age must make 4 to 6 holes on the edges of the plate. Allow the child to weave a yarn piece through the button as well as through the hole of the plate. Knot it tight to secure the buttons. Let enough space in the yarn that the button will be able to hit the plate when shaken. Put buttons across your pie dish. Make sure to shake it well and you're part of the group!

Drum

Allow the child to draw on the piece of paper. The paper can be used to cover the oatmeal bowl. Be sure that the paper is well-glued or secured with tape. An unharpened, new pencil can be a good drumstick, or the child could play with their hands to beat the drum with an tom-tom in order to maintain the time.

Horn

It's not much more simple than this. Your child can decorate toilet paper and roll of paper towels. It is possible to hang streamers or ribbons at one end. It is natural to the majority of us. What person can resist the sound of an empty roll of paper towels?

Maracas

Take off the labels on empty drink bottles made of plastic. Based on the size of the bottle make use of the funnel to put 1/4-1/2 cup of rice or beans in the bottle. Apply glue to the outside of the bottle's opening and close it securely. Beans will make an acoustic that is different and more powerful in comparison to the rice.

Guitar or Harp

Make the children decorate their shoeboxes. After removing the lid put rubber bands on the box. Make an oval cut in the top of the shoebox, and secure it with tape. Kids are able to "strum" their guitar through the round hole on upper part of the shoebox.

Story Acting

My children have always enjoyed acting out various things. Then we would read the book and somebody would do the story. Children enjoy putting their the actions into the words. Encourage your children and peers to act as characters in a story they love as you narrate. Choose a story they are familiar with and that is a constant story with consistent characters. The story should also be relatively brief. The nursery rhymes and the Aesop fables are great for this. Nicholas and Libby particularly enjoyed playing The Tortoise and the Hare in our backyard. As they aged, our children made funny videos for us that are still enjoyable to watch.

The bonds that we build with our loved ones make our lives memorable.

The ability to build strong relationships as well as the capacity to nurture them and grow these relationships is among the greatest qualities we can impart to our kids. It is not always easy to invite to another family is something I don't want to do. It's great because when I do it the invite, everyone enjoys our family time so much. It is important to be reminded that friendships can make a life truly memorable. I am reminded of the lessons that the people I have met in my life been able to teach me, as well as the time I spent with them regardless of whether their home was clean or how delicious the food we enjoyed. Do not get bogged down with the minutiae of arranging activities. Unpredictability is the key to great moments. The way we live our lives has been so scheduled that spontaneous gatherings can be delightful. Be a blessing to the people God has put around you. Your family, as well as them will be incredibly grateful that you reached out to them.

Silly Stuff

There are times where nothing goes as we had planned. Children seem to be agitated and uncooperative. The equipment is not functioning properly. The weather is awful. The mood in your home is miserable! It's time to get rid of everything and have a good time. This chapter's ideas have saved my life several times. Sometimes, we must put aside our efforts to swim ahead. We should change our direction to enjoy the view as we swim down the river.

Rainy Day Celebration

Cold or rainy days can be great occasions for having fun and comfortable times. These are also days where moms and children get a bit agitated. Here are some ideas for a positive atmosphere to help both in and out.

Indoor Picnic

Take a picnic lunch with you and stroll around the property to find the ideal location for your picnic. Place an old cloth or blanket on the floor, and then take a bite to eat. Encourage your kids to imagine that you are at the water or in the park. Imagine what you would see or be doing as if you were in the park.

Animal Safari

Find stuffed animals all over the home, under the beds, in furniture, behind closets and cupboards that you aren't worried about children getting in. Assemble with them to talk about the wild world of. Shut off all lighting and allow them to make use of a flashlight through the jungle to photograph all of the animals.

Crazy Maze

Kids love crawling around and around objects. You can create a maze around your home with items like laundry baskets, furniture, pillows, furniture cushions and toys stuffed with stuffed animals - everything you own. Use empty containers to make tunnels for your maze. Check if your kids can traverse the maze within the time frame you specify. My sister and I were young, we would play with the number of toys we could fit through the maze and not drop them. It was not clear what it would take to prepare me in bringing all things from the grocery store into the home when I became a mother.

Camping in the Great Indoors

On rainy days my children love playing indoor camping. The first time we made tents was with blankets that we draped over a few chairs, or even a table. Our next rainy day, we experimented with ropes connected to doorknobs that were in opposite rooms and then draped sheets over it. The designs are endless and the goal is to provide them with a warm quiet space. Put cereal in bags of paper for the purpose of a "campfire snack." Don't not forget to bring a torch. Sarah enjoyed setting up her home by putting up blankets, pillows as well as books, dolls and even her family cat.

Indoor S'mores

One of the best snacks for camping is S'mores. And you are able to make them for small people without having a campfire.

To make each S'more, you'll need to:

2 Graham crackers

1 marshmallow

1 tiny piece of chocolate

Then top the cracker with marshmallow and chocolate. Set it down on a paper towel and microwave at high for about 10 seconds or until the marshmallow begin to puff up. It is then covered with the second cracker and press lightly. It is possible to make a different variation using the same recipe with chocolate crackers instead of the pieces of chocolate.

Outside the House

The rainy days are among our most favorite occasions to head out to our local library. Enjoy a comfortable corner in the children's area when you've picked something from the adult shelf or pick up a magazine you want for browsing. The library has a collection of computers that offer children's programming as well as a weekly story time. Explore what our library can offer.

If it's cool enough walking through the drizzle. Even if it's raining outside, does not mean that you have to stay at home the rain all of the time. Bring every family member (including you) the bright rain slicker as well as a pair of boots to experience the thrill of splashing around in the water puddles. If you can get out even for fifteen to thirty minutes could make a difference in your mood.

Backward Day

Following a particularly stressful day, I informed Nick and Libby that on the following day I would take everything in reverse and hoping it would go more successful than what I had experienced today. In the morning, I was met with a pleasant surprise. My kids were taken serious. Nick dropped down with all of his clothes worn backwards. Libby asked what was the backward day and what would be for dinner in lieu of breakfast. The excitement of the kids prompted me to let my guard down and be part of the excitement. The group ate breakfast for dinner and wore our clothes in reverse and cleaned our teeth prior to eating food, had dessert before dinner and then played prior to the chores. It was a lot of amusement and provided me with the motivation to justify how we behave in the way we perform them.

Color Day

Have you ever thought about what the impact of color has an individual's mood? There are bright hues, soothing colors and soothing hues. What better way to plan your timetable around one color that will help to establish the mood for your loved ones? The colors of yellow or red are excellent way to lift your spirits on a grey day. Ask your kids to go through their wardrobes and dress in the appropriate color. If it is a day of red, children can sketch pictures of items that are red. Lunch may include macaroni or meatballs with tomato sauce, or tomato soup. Serve cherry or cranberry punch. Add strawberries Jell-O to serve as dessert. Make use of red construction paper to make tablecloths. The color doesn't matter you choose to use, adding a splash of colour to your day can bring joy to the mind of the entire family.

Chapter 7: Rainbow Scavenger Hunt

Kids love scavenger hunts. It's fun to uncover something earlier than any other person is an exciting experience. This easy color hunt is great for children who are just starting out. Each child is assigned a colour and ask him the child to search for up to ten things which have the color of the object. Another option is to hand your child a piece of paper that have each colour of the rainbow in the paper. You must find items that match each slip of paper, and then place it into a laundry basket. Scavenger hunts can be great for mothers as they take between 10 and 30 minutes. All kinds of lollipops can be great reward for players when the hunt has been completed.

Art Show

We all love making objects. Children love coloring, drawing, painting with tools, stamps and cutting paste as well as playing with play dough and constructing with blocks. Also, they love receiving appreciation for their hard work. Libby was well-known for putting little artifacts around the home to Jim as well as me to look for. It hurts her whenever we don't recognize her talents. The worst part is when she finds out that the frightened thought of throwing the rest of it away. It's not realistic to save every piece of paper that she has left for us. There was only so much that we could share with grandma, and the uncles and aunts. We opted to put on an exhibition of her art. She displayed her art and let her decide which pieces were her favorites. The pieces were then added to the "blue ribbon" collection. Blue ribbons are kept in a storage box located in the attic of her home for her. The concept of an art exhibition proved a huge success and inspired Nick to try some different creative ideas that he had created on his own. We also took pictures of his block-building creations for the show to include in our exhibits.

Art Displays

These are creative and exciting ways to show your artwork with your kids:

For a simple evening art show, place your child's photos on the table, then cover the table with clear plastic. The table will be set to eat dinner in the same way as always. While everyone is eating their meals, allow kids share their thoughts on each photograph.

If you own an outdoor clothing line, you could build an outdoor gallery. Attach your child's clothespins on the clothesline. Families and friends are able to stroll between the rows of art and have fun.

* A family I know have a rotating display of art in their fridge. Get some cheap, light frame and a piece of magnet tape (available in craft stores). Children can decorate the frames. You could write each child's name within the frame. The artwork of children can be displayed within their frame at the door of your refrigerator. Each week let

them select their most favorite piece from the previous week and then replace previous week's choices.

It is possible to take photos of all the work of your child, and save your photos inside a unique art album. This is an excellent option for people with limited area and will cherish this memory for a long time.

Pet Birthday

The idea of celebrations for a pet's birthday could appear absurd to some people and yet this book is titled "Silly Stuff." When we first began celebrating the birthday of a pet, we were unsure of the date that our dog's birthday was therefore I chose one day in the month of January. The reason I chose January was because it is typically the month that everyone is suffering from the symptoms of cabin fever and require some sort of celebration.

We made a special dessert we played games, enjoyed cake and our dog receives cookies, cards as well as lots of love.

Puppy Chow (for people)

The first time I had tried it was at the church potluck supper. The adults and kids alike enjoyed the idea.

In order to make one batch, you'll be required to:

1. Cup of Chocolate Chips

One cup peanut butter (smooth)

14 lb margarine or butter

8 cups of Chex cereal

2 Cups powdered sugar

In a large bowl that is microwave safe, Melt the chocolate chips butter and peanut butter in the microwave for approximately two minutes. Add cereal and mix the cereal thoroughly. Put the mix inside a grocery bag made of paper and sprinkle with powdered sugar. Shake to coat, then serve.

Kitty Lunch

It is possible to make adorable "mice" to celebrate a cat's day of celebration.

It is also possible to serve Swedish Fish candies for a snack.

Each mouse will require:

Half of a roll that is hard

tuna salad

Carrot slices

M&M candies

licorice laces

Hollow out half a soft roll and fill it up with tuna salad. Make use of the slices of carrot for mice's ears. M&M for eyes and nose, and liquorice to make whiskers, and also an tail.

At the time of your pet's birthday celebration If you're feeling ridiculous, let your children pour their drink out of small bowls.

Circus

We certainly couldn't forget some of the exciting activities we've attempted at the circus that it has dreamed up. It's a fantastical and exotic, sparkling place that children like to mimic the experience. This is why the circus is so well-known since more than 200 years.

Costumes

The time has come to get the makeup and costumes box. Each child should decide on the character they'll be playing in their performance. The ringmaster could sport an ersatz mustache on the handlebar and there could also be lions, tigers, bears, clowns, and, of course, clowns. The process of getting them dressed could take time. Allow them to enjoy the game to the extent that they are attracted.

Make extravagant headbands and hats that resemble trapeze performers. Include plenty of beads, feathers, and even stones that they can glue on pieces made of construction paper. The construction paper should be glued in an arc that wraps around the head like crowns.

If the kids are dressed to impress, set up some fun music, and then make a parade of costumes around the yard or house. Once the parade is finished, do not forget to provide snacks like animal crackers or popcorn as well as lemonade.

It is a great idea to encourage your children to create their own versions of the circus. The kids can play animals, perform some slapstick tumbling, and even run around on an imaginary high wire. Spend the time and take in their shows. For the 10 minutes or so that it takes to show kids this kind of attention (don't overlook the applause!) helps increase their self-confidence.

Western Round-Up - Pioneers

In the past, many individuals have been enthralled by this aspect of the Old West. When you're struggling you can use this fascination to benefit you? Put on family clothes such as coats and hats, so they'll pretend to be taking a ride on the Range. It has been my experience that when I read stories for my kids with props and a few toys, their imaginations are kept active. Consider reading a few stories of tall tales like Pecos Bill, Paul Bunyon or John Henry. The fictional characters could inspire imagination-inspiring play on America's growth. Children's books are available on popular Americans who paved the way for opening up the west such as Daniel Boone and Davy Crockett. The librarian in your area can help to find books for children that is related to the themes I've listed in this collection. Our goal is to stay with biographies and classics. This way we're helping our kids learn about the past and of literature.

Cowboy Grub

Serve hot dogs cut into pieces with beans served on an aluminum pie plate and an item of bread that has been buttered. It is important to cut hotdog slices into half to avoid the hotdogs from choking. Kids can relax in a circle, on the surface to eat their hotdogs, as the cowpokes ate out at the Range.

Campfire Sing-a-long

There is no need for a campfire to sing-along. It is possible to share the songs at the campfire with your children. If you're not aware of some "cowboy" songs try teaching your children patriotic tunes such as "This Land is My Land," or "America the Beautiful." Nicholas's top choice song was "Happy Trails to You." Children are awestruck by singing and hearing their tiny singing voices can be a delight to parents of any age. It's fun recording them and replay it a second time.

Story-telling Read Alouds

Singing stories and listening to stories is an enjoyable pastime. The experience is more enjoyable especially when you do it beneath the stars or inside the blanket of a fort, pretending that you're on the wagon train that is traveling towards Dakota. Dakota territory. A few of our most loved tales of the pioneers come from The Little House of the Praire by Laura Ingalls Wilder. Our family is also amazed by the journeys of Lewis and Clark.

Cars, Trains, and Airplanes

As Nick as well as Libby were young, I observed a fundamental difference between the two. Libby provided every toy with an individuality and connection to any other toy. It was balls or dolls, there was two parents and a child. Nick however, in contrast provided everything with a motor by making a sound. Each toy, be it a car or toy animal was now motorized. It was an extremely intriguing study. Instead of trying to fight his love affair with mechanicals that I built, I adapted the fascination. I'm not surprised for me that he's currently a pilot who is flying all over the world.

Create a Vehicle

Sometimes, you can take home a cardboard container from your local grocer's. Inspire your child to create their own train, car or perhaps an aircraft. Make sure you fold the sides of the box to ensure that your child is able to rest within the box. Bring crayons, colored paper and glue so you can make your car more attractive. Paper pie plates are great wheels as well as a steering wheel. The wings can be made from those flaps that are on the boxes.

After their car is complete, give them a map and then ask your child to tell you what they're going to do. You could "map" out their route. Go to Google maps to plan travel plans. Use flightaware.com for a look at the air travel routes. Provide your guests with a meal to enjoy their journey as well as a hug and promise to see them upon their return from their fantasy trip. Kids love it when parents join with them in their imaginary world.

• Help your child grow in their imagination.

I have friends who prefer to buy a new toy their child rather than confront the complexities that comes with making a toy. Do not give into this desire. Children must go through the creation process. When they utilize their imagination to construct a vehicle or tent, they learn. This helps them develop the ability to make decisions. It increases their confidence and self-confidence. They will gain experience of solving issues. This is among the fundamental skills that they'll require to be successful in adulthood. Parents who allow their children to grow in their creative abilities, they're investing in their child's future. Wouldn't this be worth the trouble?

Planned Attacks on Boredom

Did you notice anticipation leading up to an event can be just more fun than the actual event? It's incredible the effect that a bright red circle on the calendar could have. It gives us motivation and also offers an opportunity to anticipate. It is important to incorporate events into our calendars so that I don't end up becoming boring. Also, I need to keep my life more interesting. We moms love to discover new facts about history and to share them with family members. This chapter's suggestions will be most effective if you prepare them in advance of the dates given. Select and pick the suggestions which appeal to you as well as your kids. Try not to try the entire list in one go otherwise the excitement will wear off. However, I'll warn that any concept you attempt could become so popular you'll be forced to repeat the idea for a long time to be. Be simple. These ideas are found within encyclopedias, calendars or in the library. It is possible to find new ones to add this list. I made an effort not to list prominent holidays or events. It felt more exciting to honor the less well-known. When I begin each month, I make an effort to select one or two events to fit into our calendar.

January

It is the month that where I have to think of something special planned. There is no actual holiday that I am looking forward to, and the joy of Christmas has slowed down.

January 8 - Singer Elvis Presley's Birthday (1935)

Listen to some of Elvis's best hit songs while doing your house tidying.

January 9 - First U.S. Balloon Flight (1793)

Get a helium balloon, and test whether your children are able to get it floating across the room, without touching it.

January 11 - International Thank You Day

Encourage your kids to write Thank you cards for the individuals in your life who are special to you. Visit the post office to send the notes.

January 18 - Author A.A. Milne's Birthday (1882)

It is a good idea to read Winnie the Pooh and the Blustery Day while you snack on honey and biscuits. (*Do not feed honey to a baby less than 2 years old.)

January 22 - National Popcorn Day

Make some fresh toppings for the popcorn in a large bowl.

Sprinkle your the popcorn bowl with Parmesan cheese, or any other spice.

Microwave Caramel Popcorn

For six cups of caramel popcorn,, you will require:

6 cups of popcorn that has been popped

Half cup almonds(optional)

1/4 cup of tightly packed brown sugar

2 tablespoons light corn syrup

1/2 cup margarine, or butter

1 teaspoon baking soda

1/8 teaspoon of salt.

Make popcorn with almonds in a large, microwave-safe bowl. In a microwave-safe bowl, mix brown sugar as well as corn syrup, butter or margarine, as well as salt. The microwave should be on high for two minutes, then stir. Continue to microwave on high for 2 to 3 minutes or until mixture is brought to a boiling. Stir in baking soda. Sprinkle over the Almonds and popcorn. Mix until coated. Make popcorn by microwave at high for two minutes. Spread it on waxed papers to be cool. Enjoy!

Popcorn Balls

It is also possible to use buttered hands to rapidly and effectively make balls from the mix. Cover each ball with plastic wrap.

December 24 - The discovery of gold within California (1848)

Place some pennies, water and sand into an empty dish-basin. Use kitchen strainers for the children and let them cook to collect shiny pennies. It is possible to clean your pennies so they shine, by immersing them in a mix of vinegar and baking soda.

January 26 - Australia Day (1788)

Let your kids pretend to be kangaroos, and have them try the shrimp "barbie" for dinner.

February

The month of February is one of the most short in the calendar, yet it's packed with exciting activities to take in. Some of the most well-known commemorative holidays include Ground Hog Day, St. Valentine's Day, Presidents' Day and Martin Luther King Day. Additionally, it's Black History and Dental Health Month.

February 4 - Aviator Charles Lindbergh's Birthday (1902)

Explore a smaller regional airport and see planes take off and then land.

February 7 - Author Laura Ingalls Wilder's Birthday (1867)

Celebrate pioneer life. Explore the pages of Little House in the Big Woods the very first of Laura Ingalls Wilder's fantastic novels. Have a delicious cornbread and homemade butter.

Cornbread

To make 9 servings, you'll be required to:

1 cup all-purpose flour,

1 cup of cornmeal

2 tablespoons of sugar

Four teaspoons baking powder

1 cup milk

1/4 cup oil or shortening melted

1 egg slightly beat.

Preheat the oven until 425° F. In an ice cream maker, combine cornmeal, flour as well as sugar and baking powder. Add milk, oil and eggs. Mix by hand until it is smooth. Put the batter in a greased 8 or 9-inch pan. Bake for 18 to 22 minutes, or until a toothpick poked into the cake emerges clear.

Homemade Butter

You'll need:

A small container with lid (a Baby food jar is great)

Chapter 8: Heavy Whipping Cream

Place the cream into the jar and leave room at the top. Cover the lid tightly. Your child should hold the jar with two hands, and then shake it. Continue shaking until small pieces of butter appear. If your child becomes exhausted, let them hand over the container to a different person who will shake it. Once the butter chunks appear, pour them into the bowl. Add some salt sprinkles If you like. Sprinkle the butter over warm cornbread.

There is also the option of making butter with a mixer. My father and I came across this when we were making whipping cream to decorate a cake. The cream was too thick and we found sweet butter.

February 9 - U.S. Weather Bureau Began Operations (1870)

Discuss weather issues together with your children. What is the definition of weather? How will it affect us? Get an affordable outdoor thermometer. Let children help them create their own weather forecasts. Watch the weather reports on the radio and find out how precise they are.

February 11 - National Inventor's Day - Thomas Edison's Birthday (1847)

Give examples of items we have in our home, which Thomas Edison helped to create. Invite children to think up something that they can come up with their own. Give them pencils and paper for children to draw their ideas. Play dough, straws or popsicle sticks, any things you are able to provide, help them create a model of their creation.

February 26 - Buffalo Bill Cody's Birthday (1846)

To commemorate the birthday of the Wild West Show founder, let your kids make the cowboy's vests with fringes from paper grocery bags.

Cowboy Vests

Each vest will require:

1 grocery bag made of paper

scissors, crayons

construction paper

glue

Cut the grocery bag across the middle, allowing to allow for openings in the vest. On the top of the bag, cut the hole to fit the neck of your child. Along the sides of the bag make armholes. Then, turn the vest upside down in a way that the interior of the bag can be seen. Encourage your child to embellish their vest with as much color as they can with crayons, colored papers, as well as glue.

March

The month of March in our region of the world is an extremely windy and turbulent month that is completely unpredictably in terms of weather related. It is a great time to go outside and fly kites. Winter isn't over however, which is why I make an effort to keep a variety of indoor pursuits in the back of my mind in case of those snowy days that are the last day of winter.

March 2 - Author Dr. Suess' Birthday (1904)

Put on silly hats and read the most loved Dr. Suess books. Include green food coloring in scrambled eggs, and then enjoy it along with ham that has been fried.

March 3 - Inventor Alexander Graham Bell's Birthday (1847)

Paper Cup Telephone

Create a phone using string and two cups. Create a hole through the cup's bottom. run at least one of the strings into the cup's bottom and tie it with knots. The string should be stretched out, then secure it. Discuss with your child on your "wire."

Telephone Game

Your children should form a line in one row. Make a joke or rhyme to the very first child who is in the row. Let the kids relay the message to the next child in the line, whispering it into the ear of the child next. What was the change in message since the last child was exposed to the message? Be sure to give clear and concise messages.

March 8 - Author Kenneth Grahame's Birthday (1859)

Find a comfy spot and take in Kenneth Grahame's amazing tales in The Wind and the Willows

March 11 - Johnny Appleseed Day

Tell the American popular tale about Johnny Appleseed. Dress in hats and pots. Have a cup of apple sauce, caramel apples and apple pie.

Applesauce

To make 6 servings, you'll be required to:

6-8 apples cored, peeled and chopped

1 cup of sugar

1 teaspoon of cinnamon (optional)

In a large pan, cook the apples on low heat for 15 to 20 mins or until the apples are tender. Removing from the warmth. Add cinnamon and sugar. Mix thoroughly. With a fork or potato masher to mash the apple mixture. Allow to cool before enjoying.

Caramel Apples

Buy some caramel sauce to use to make Ice cream sundaes. Cut and core the apple slices. Warm the caramel sauce in a small dish in the microwave in accordance with directions on the packaging. Let the kids dip the apple slices in the caramel sauce.

March 12 - U.S. Post Office Established (1789)

Visit the local post office to ask if they can offer your children the opportunity to go on a visit.

March 19 - Missionary/Explorer David Livingstone's Birthday (1813)

Explore missionaries and the things they accomplish. Make cards with your kids or photos to mail an individual missionary that the church is supporting. This is also a wonderful day to have a play with stuffed animals safari.

March 24 - The First Automobile Sold in the U.S. (1898)

Visit the local dealership for cars and enjoy your family taking a look at the different cars. What kind of vehicle best suits your personality and the style member of your family? Do you have a mom who drives an Mustang or dad an Ford pickup?

March 31 - The Eiffel Tower Completed (1889)

Your children are invited to create the tallest tower they could. Give them some building supplies including empty cardboard boxes or pillows. You can also provide canned veggies.

April

April showers are bringing May blooms. In the meantime, you're waiting for the rains to cease and for the flowers to blossom you can try these things.

April 2 - Author Hans Christian Anderson's Birthday (1805)

Read the Ugly Duckling and invite your kids to play the story while you read. Let them create their own story.

April 4 - First U.S. Flag Approved (1818)

Offer your child the American Flag or a photo of one. With a set of paper, white, red and blue crayons, help your child to create a unique flag for the family.

April 9 - America's First Public Library Established (1833)

You must visit the library! If you aren't able to go out on a Saturday, this is the perfect time to sort through your collection, and build an individual library.

April 20 - Make a Quilt Day

Each child should be given an activity book or paper. Ask children to draw or color on the page. The students must color intensely and then press the crayons. After they have finished coloring then place them with the crayons facing down on the fabric. Each image will form the size of a square in your quilt. Press a hot iron down on the image you have drawn. The crayons melt in the fabric, and then transfer an image mirror-like on the fabric. After all the images have been applied, you can sew edges around the cloth to prevent it from becoming frayed. You can use the material as an ornament for the wall.

April 26 - Naturalist J.J. Audubon's Birthday (1785)

Find out what kinds of birds are in your yard while you prepare yummy snacks for your feathered companions.

Birdseed Snack

To make each birdeed snack, you'll require:

1 pinecon

Peanut butter

birdseed

String

The activity can be messy, so when it's warm, you can do this in the outdoors. With a spoon, children should put peanut butter on their pinecone. Place the bird's seed in a bowl large enough to give each child the opportunity to fill their pinecones with seeds by rolling the seed. Connect a string to every pinecone to hang it from an adjacent tree.

May

The time is now to go outside and enjoy the outdoors. Make sure to take a walk during the warmer days. Be aware that any exercise you perform inside could be accomplished outside, too.

May 1 - Mother Goose Day

Your child can learn Mother Goose rhymes. Recite them at the end of dinner time for your whole family.

May 2, 1936 - Peter and the Wolf premiered in Moscow (1936)

This amazing composition can be a wonderful way introduce your kids to orchestra. This recording is very popular for us at family. Help your kids imagine that you are one of the characters of the story as they listen to the music that is appropriate.

May 7 - Composers Johann Brahm's (1833) and Peter Tchaikovsky's Birthdays (1840)

The two gentlemen graced the world with their most stunning music. They evoke the images of dances and lullabies. Begin to introduce your child to the soothing sounds from classical music.

May 14 - Lewis and Clark Expedition Began (1804)

Today is the time to go for a walk in the pace of a toddler. Take a snack with you and check out what's happening in your community. Be patient and don't hurry to reach your destination and just wander around.

May 16 - Biographers Day

Encourage your child to tell their tale. By using a tape recorder, you can ask your child unanswered questions about their experiences. They'll love listening to the tape in 10 years.

May 18 - Mt. St. Helens Erupted (1980)

Let your child construct the largest mountain using clay. Create a hole at the summit of the mountain that is large enough to accommodate a disposable cup. Inside the cup, mix one tablespoon baking soda, and one teaspoon of vinegar. Watch the volcano burst into flames.

June

June is Fresh Fruit and Vegetable Month. If you're able to, make use of the pick-your-own strawberry farms. Make enough for homemade strawberry jam. In January, you'll have the flavor of summer waiting to be enjoyed.

Strawberry Freezer Jam

In order to make 5 cups jam, you'll need:

1 quart or 2 pints of strawberries

Four cups of sugar

1 Cup of Water

1 box powdered fruit pectin

Clean the strawberries and then hull them. In a large bowl, let your children smash them with an potato masher, or fork. Mix in the sugar, and allow to the mixture sit for about for 10 minutes. In a small pan, combine the fruit pectin with water. Bring to a boil and cook for one minute while mixing continuously. Mix pectin into the the fruit mix. Mix for 3 minutes until it dissolves all of the sugar. Scoop into clean jars or freezer containers, leaving 1 inch headspace. Then cool and then cover tightly-fitting lids. Allow to set for up to 24 hours. You can store it in your freezer up to a year, or store in your refrigerator for two to three weeks.

June 3 - Casey at the Bat Published (1888)

Find a copy of the classic poem, and read it to your kids.

June 8 - Ice Cream First Sold in the U.S. (1786)

You can try making your own ice cream.

Tin Can Ice Cream

For making one batch of vanilla ice cream, the following ingredients are required:

1 cup milk

1 cup of heavy cream

1 cup of sugar

1 teaspoon vanilla

A small amount of salt

Clean and dry 12 ounce coffee container and 1 fresh and dry, 39-ounce can of coffee with lids that fit tight.

rock salt

Ice

Mix together in a large bowl the cream, milk, vanilla, sugar, as well as a pinch of salt. Stir until sugar is dissolved. The mix should be poured into the coffee container smaller and close the lid tight. Place the smaller container inside the larger container and place crushed ice on top. Sprinkle rock salt on the ice before snapping the lid to the bigger can.

Your children should move the can around between each of. Within 15 minutes, take off the lid of the bigger can, and then drain the water. Lift the lid of the smaller container and mix the mixture of ice cream that is thickening. Replace the lid. You can add more salt and ice to the can that is larger and put on a new lid. Let the kids to roll the can around for 10 minutes more.

Ice creams will be soft and tasty.

June 12 - First Baseball Game Played in the U.S. (1839)

Bring the whole family out to play a ball game. Make hotdogs and sandwiches for the lunch.

July

The most popular summer and august activities include having fun in the sandbox or the swimming pool. There are other things you can try on those scorching and cloudy summer days.

July 5 - Phineas T. Barnum's Birthday (1810)

P.T. Barnum is perhaps best famous for his circus however did you know that Barnum also developed his town Bridgeport CT., owned an industrial clock company as well as built a number of nature museums? Let your children create your own museum with their toys, stuffed animals and small knick-knacks. Take them for a tour.

July 7 - Chocolate Day, Chocolate Introduced in Europe (1550)

It's the perfect day to indulge in delicious chocolate desserts.

Chocolate Brownies

To make 2 dozen brownies, you'll need:

1-2/3 cups sugar

1-1/2 sticks melted margarine

2 tablespoons of water

2 eggs

2 teaspoons vanilla

1 1/3 cups of flour

3/4 cup of unsweetened cocoa

1 teaspoon baking powder

Preheat oven to 350 ° F. Combine sugar, margarine that has been melted as well as water in an enormous bowl. Add vanilla, eggs, and the vanilla. Add cocoa, flour, as well as baking powder. Mix thoroughly. Place the mixture in a greased 13x9-inch baking pan. Bake for 18 to 25 mins and until the toothpick emerges slightly sticky. Let it cool in the pan.

July 9 - Donut Cutter Invented (1872)

Visit the bakery of your choice or to a donut shop and have a blast!

July 11 - Author, E.B. White's Birthday (1899)

Read E.B. White's fantastic masterpiece Charlotte's Web. Go with your children to the fairgrounds and visit the animals.

July 13 - International Puzzle Day

Once you've worked on an enjoyable puzzle Let the children create their own.

Personal Puzzle

Each puzzle will require:

1 piece of cardboard or an oak tag

Crayons or markers

scissors

Allow each child to create and color their own picture on the oak or cardboard tag. The finished art work can be cut into pieces of puzzle. Combine the pieces to see how long it will take to put it all back in place. It is possible to create a more difficult collage by choosing the theme of your choice, for example the animals or flowers. Take pictures from magazines or download them from the web and paste them onto cardboard. Photos of family members can be used to create truly personal games.

July 19 - Ice Cream Day

Another day dedicated to the ice cream! Create an ice cream Sundae fixer bar for dinner tonight. Include strawberry sauce, chocolate sauce preserves, caramel topping sprinkles and whipped cream bananas, cherries, as well as crushed candy bars. Make sure you tailor the selections to your loved ones' tastes.

July 28 - Author Beatrix Potter's Birthday (1866)

If you've not done it recently, now is the ideal time to introduce your children to Peter Rabbit Beatrix Potter's delightful classic.

August

August 5 - Astronaut Neil Armstrong's Birthday (1930)

To celebrate Neil Armstrong's birthday, let the children stay up until midnight. Place blankets on the lawn and gaze at the night sky. They can imagine how it would feel to be flying through the space.

August 9 - Smokey the Bear's Birthday (1944)

Have a discussion about safety in the kitchen with your kids. Inform them about the risks associated with playing with matches and cooking on the stove. It is important to teach them what to do in the event there is an incident of flame. Practice an escape plan.

August 19 - National Aviation Day, Orville Wright's Birthday (1871)

Create paper planes and fly these in your backyard. Check out the model that can fly the most far, the most unique and is the longest lasting.

August 21 - Hawaii Became 50th State (1959)

To celebrate our 50th anniversary, state, treat your family and friends to pineapples and then teach them to hula dance.

Easy Pineapple Upside Down Cake

To make one cake, you'll require:

1 cup of brown sugar

1/4 cup margarine, melted, or butter

6 slices of pineapple from canned cans

6 maraschino cherries(optional)

1/4 cup of pineapple juice(you could also use the juice of canning pineapple slices)

1 box of yellow cake mix

Pre-heat the oven at 350° F. In an unassuming bowl mix margarine and brown sugar. The mixture should be spread in the bottom of the 9-inch rectangular cake pan. Place the slices of pineapple and maraschino cherries on top of the brown sugar mix. Mix cake batter according to instructions on the box, but reduce the amount of water to 1/4 cup. Include 1/4 cup of pineapple juice into the cake mix. The prepared mix should be placed in the pan and cover with pineapple slices and cherries. Bake for between 30 and 35 minutes or until a sharp toothpick is clean when inserted. Allow to cool in the pan for two minutes. Place on a serving dish.

August 24 - National Park Service Established (1916)

Make plans for a picnic at the local park. Also, you can watch a film about an National Park from your library and then watch it with your family.

September

It's over and the older siblings are at the school. You can now spend some quiet time with your younger youngsters. Enjoy!

September 11 - Writer O. Henry's Birthday (1862)

Our most loved O. Henry story is The Gift of the Magi. There are many beautifully illustrated versions that you can discuss with your children. Encourage them to think of a thing they have that they would sacrifice for someone other.

September 13 - International Chocolate Day

There is never enough chocolate.

Chapter 9: Chocolate Dipped Pretzels

If you want to indulge in a sweet treat, you'll need:

1 bag of semi-sweet or white chocolate chips or milk chocolate chip

One bag of pretzel rods.

The chocolate chips should be melted in the microwave-safe bowl. The kids can dip the an end of pretzel rods in the chocolate. The chocolate should be allowed to sit until the pretzels set and then harden on waxed paper prior to eating.

September 14, 1714 Francis Scott Key wrote the "Star-Spangled Banner" (1814)

Instruct your toddler to sing the National Anthem. The flag is a topic to discuss and its meaning. Instruct your children about that the Pledge of Allegiance.

September 19 - Walt Disney Produced the First "Talking" Cartoon (1928)

I'm not usually a fan of viewing videos, however today could be an ideal time to hire the classic Disney classic such as Snow White or Sleeping Beauty. If you're not a fan of princesses, consider Steamboat Willie.

September 25 - Explorer Balboa Discovered the Pacific Ocean (1513)

If you're not able to visit the sea today, let it let its energy fill your home. The kids can spread the towels across the floor, dress in swimming suits and make up a scene of the beach.

October

There's plenty to do during October. Enjoy the variety of autumn activities available. Pumpkin picking is a popular option, as are the hayrides. Don't forget about leaping into huge piles of autumn leaves. It's fun to sweep leaves, and then make an adorable nest within the middle. Bring a few blankets, some cider, as well as donuts to have snacks in your cozy leaves.

October 23 - Athlete Pele's Birthday (1940)

When you've finished raking the leaves, bring the kids together for a soccer game on the grass in celebration of the birthplace of soccer's most famous player.

October 25 - Johann Strauss' Birthday (1825)

Strauss was the King of the Waltz. So why not show the younger youngsters this dance?

October 27 - Navy Day

Make a fleet of boats and launch them into the tub.

November

The months of November and December are exhilarating filled with activity and they don't need to add any. We all need some time to unwind from the holiday stress. Use these easy ideas to take a break from your busy schedule.

November 3 - Sandwich Day, Sandwich Invented (1762)

Find a variety of bread, such as wheat, rye, or French and mix them with vegetables, meats and other condiments for an appetizer buffet at dinner. Allow your children to make their own versions of a perfect sandwich. Make sure to include pickles on the side.

November 14 - Artist Claude Monet's Birthday (1840)

Monet is one of the artists that Libby loves most. Her fascination is with his colors, and the beautiful flowers. So why not let your new artist make a masterpiece for the day of her birth anniversary?

November 18 - The First Teddy Bear's Birthday (1902)

Put a picnic table on the floor. Send invitations to the bears at home, and then have a teddy bear picnic. The event is fun for all ages and cleanup is simple; you just need to shake the blanket. You can read Goldilocks as well as The Three Bears to your children and furry companions.

December

December 3 - Galileo Perfected the Telescope (1621)

The December sky is usually crystal clean. You can wake your children up at darkness and let them go outside for a night-time stargaze. This will be one of those unforgettable moments that they'll remember for the rest of their life.

December 9 - Christmas Cards Created (1843)

Bring out the crayons, papers or pencils. as well as help your children create your own Christmas cards that they can deliver to relatives and friends.

December 30 - Author Rudyard Kipling's Birthday (1865)

Kids love Kiplings adorable The Jungle Book. The book is an ideal option to relax following a day of Christmas.

• Make the events that you organize for your children to be interesting to you as well.

It's not easy to be motivated enough to create things for your kids. From a mature perspective it is more exciting to find other options to entertain yourself than with Matchbox toys or cars. Find motives to organize things that you are interested in. Kids can tell if we do not want to be playing with their toys. Look for things that you are enthusiastic about and share with your children. The enthusiasm you have will spread and you'll become kids who are more cooperative and tolerant.

Children are an amazing present God has bestowed to us. Being a parent is an honor and an opportunity. Family time into our plans and give it the highest top priority. A visit to the dry cleaning shop is significantly more enjoyable if you're able to take having a picnic at the park. It's more thrilling to get up in the morning and say, "Today is Inventor's Day," instead of saying "Oh another Monday." Include unique events within your daily schedule. They will not just benefit your family, but will also be a blessing for your own family too.

Fun on the Run

Everyone has been in the restaurant eating a meal and children sitting next to us begins to scream. When I was a child I would have been annoyed me, but now I have immense empathy for the mother of this child. I understand how difficult it can be to know that everyone at a medical office, supermarket or restaurant public space is watching the child to help them get to be under control. This chapter will help you be ready for these situations and the best way to prepare before time to reduce the likelihood of them. It's not possible to guarantee that these suggestions can solve all instances of anxiety and annoyance, but the presence of a plan will help. Similar to an Girl Scout, moms need to be always well-prepared.

Chapter 10: Boredom Basics

The term "boredom" is used to describe a situation that is defined by the perception that one's surroundings are as boring, dull or lacking in excitement. The reason for this could be due to the lack of leisure or interest in aesthetics.

The Background

The same, work as art, can be a passive pursuit, or sunk in the monotony of life. The human condition is a source of anxiety boredom. People will exert an enormous amount of effort to prevent or alleviate it. Yet, often, it's considered to be a form of suffering that needs to endure.

The most common passive methods to get the boredom cycle is sleeping or thinking of new ideas. The most common active methods involve an intentional activity of some type, often something different because repetition and familiarity result in boredom.

Boredom can also play a part in existentialist thinking. If one feels physically or mentally confined the boredom may be addressed by various religious practices however, this is not due to the fact that religions would like to be associated with boredom, but it is because boredom can be seen as an essential human condition for which God and wisdom or morality offer the most fundamental responses. Boredom can be understood as such by almost every existentialist philosopher.

With no stimulants or concentration In the absence of stimulants or focus, the individual is confronted by the lack of meaning, and an absence of being, and is confronted with an existential tension.

Though it's not thoroughly studied, research about boredom has shown that it's an important factor that affects many parts of a person's daily life. The people who score low on the boredom proneness scale have been found to be more successful across a variety of areas of their lives which includes vocations study, self-reliance, and education.

The feeling of boredom could be a sign of depression. The condition of boredom could be a manifestation of weakness that is learned which is closely connected to depression clinical.

A few parenting theories advise that children have been raised in a space without stimulation, and not permitted or encouraged to engage with their surroundings and environment, they will not develop the capacities of their minds to do this.

Chapter 11: Why Are You Bored

It is important to determine the reason you're bored to get beyond it and come up with about more stimulating thought.

What Are the Reasons?

Do you have a plan that you've done many times before? Consider adding something different or performing it in a different method. If it doesn't work, stop doing the exact same procedure repeatedly.

If, however, repetitive jobs are element of your work, then you could be forced to make a option but to do the task.

Do you feel a bit shy exhausted, fatigued, or just plain feeling unmotivated? It is possible to reenergize yourself and may surprise you at how motivated you can experience after just a few minutes of a catnap. Also, breathing outdoors in fresh air just a few minutes can refresh your mind as well as the fresh air as well as (maybe) the sun can improve your mood.

Are you tired but in a state of slack? Do your best to convince yourself that you should take on just one small task: something that is small, shorter in length or the beginning of a project. Making small steps towards your goal could give you an experience of accomplishment that can squelch boredness.

Are you feeling bored and aren't able to do what you'd like to accomplish? It could be an difficult situation to find yourself in since the only factor that is stopping you from completing the task or having enjoyable time is the absence of resources or perhaps knowledge.

Think of alternative strategies to get the goals you're trying to achieve by using the resources you can use.

Are you bored because you are unable to think of something else to do? Get physically or socially engaging.

A few workouts can help you get into a more positive mental state and also provide an added benefit to keep you fit. Engaging in social activities (i.e. speaking to someone) is one of the fundamental human requirements. Contact with a person face-to-face is superior to talking on the phone or Facebook.

Chapter 12: Make Everyday Interesting

Every single day is a memorable day. But you're not able to be able to appreciate the significance of it. Be sure to follow these additional actions to make your day exciting and not boring routine.

Get A Grip

Enjoy your day like you would like to live it as the last. Making a list of goals for the things you'll do is great and you might even discover intriguing things before you reach the task?

Illustration: If headed to work, and you work, take a moment to take a moment to take a look around to see what's new in the city. Are there fresh buildings or retail store? You are never sure when you will have to use that store which you saw when you were driving to work.

Take a few minutes to organize your desk. There is likely to be a lot of things to accomplish, but having a desk with a mess this isn't the best option. It's not going to stop if you spend an hour cleaning your desk. It will help you work better.

Do something to help others. We often forget how self-centered we can be. It's true that you must be at work, and there are plenty of things to do, but providing a helping hand people will make you satisfied and worth the effort.

Discover something new. Each day, you have the chance to discover something you did not know about previously. Make use of the web and when you discover a new word, you'll have more than you were the previous day.

Grin. Find positive people who you can hang out with and not people whom you find toxic. People who are optimistic can affect the person around them. This is what you want in case you're feeling bored.

Perhaps you'd like to make your own guidelines for how your day will be. Based on where you are spending your day, make sure you do the things make you feel appreciated as well as appreciated whether at home or somewhere else.

Chapter 13: Be Curious

Develop your interest in the world around you and within yourself. It is boring because you are stuck in patterns of some routines or actions. Consider looking at ways to do them in a different way and find interested

in new ideas and options.

New Things

Improve your memory. A lot of what's thought of as intelligence is being able to remember things effectively. It is possible improve your ability to keep and remember memories using a range of methods, such as using the use of mnemonics, and paying greater focus on the specifics.

You can read a lot. Everything humans can comprehend is discovered in printed form, be it in magazines, books, as well as on the web. Get a love for reading, and you'll get exposed to a greater variety of ideas and facts. If you're not a fast reader consider learning how to speed read. You could consider jotting down notes, or perhaps referring to a word or two from the dictionary.

Find yourself more interested. What is the process that allows some people to comprehend so much? The ability to remember things is only one part of the solution You also have to be interested. If you're content living your life without any awareness of what you're not familiar to, you'll never be able to learn anything and will eventually become bored. Be determined to become more interested and encourage yourself to develop curiosity can broaden your perspectives and reduce boredom.

The lack of initiative in curiosity is like driving a car that's run empty of gas and won't get you anywhere.

Find out things independently. There's more to the pursuit of curiosity beyond "book smarts". We could all develop the ability to handle every day chores at home, work or school more efficiently and more effectively. If you aren't sure what you need to do you're not sure about, don't request someone else to complete it for you. Instead, let them show you how to do it yourself. Most of the time the case, you'll be able to discover the answer on your own, whether through testing and error or through research.

Exercise your brain in different ways. The majority of us excel in the areas we are excelling in through nature or routines we perform daily. Try to master new skills or think differently but you'll find yourself more relaxed. Choose something that you'd like to master (play guitar, as an example) or an area where you're not a great student (perhaps math) focus on the aspect. In the beginning, you may be unsure and even more bored than prior to, but if do your homework or work on it regularly it will make you more comfortable, and discover new ways of thinking to your thoughts.

Choose a pastime that is enjoyable to you. Most people improve their proficiency by trying to become better in something they already excel in. This not only makes your appearance smarter, but it will help you remain sane.

Connect with smart people. Becoming surrounded by people who are more knowledgeable than you are can help you to become more engaged.

www.ingramcontent.com/pod-product-compliance
Lightning Source LLC
Chambersburg PA
CBHW070554010526
44118CB00012B/1319